Mel Bay Presents

Andrés Segovia, As I Knew Him

By John W. Duarte

Andrés Segovia and John Duarte, ca. 1964 (Photo: Maurice Summerfield, courtesy *Classical Guitar Magazine*)

#4 Industrial Drive
Pacific, Missouri 63069
1-800-8-MELBAY

Andrés Segovia and Jack Duarte discuss a page from Duarte's transcription of Robert Dowland's A Varietie of Lute-Lessons. *(Photo: Maurice Summerfield, courtesy Classical Guitar Magazine)*

"This book is dedicated to those whose unfailing encouragement and support at 'key points' in my life have been central to my sixty-five years with the guitar: Andrés Segovia, Terence Usher, Len Williams, and, last but in no way least, my wife."

— John Duarte

ANDRÉS SEGOVIA, AS I KNEW HIM
John W. Duarte

©1998 by Mel Bay Publications, Inc.

Mel Bay Publications, Inc.
Pacific, MO 63069
1-800-8 MEL-BAY

Visit us on the World Wide Web at *http://www.melbay.com*
Send E-mail to us at *email@melbay.com*

ISBN 0-7866-3319-0

CONTENTS

FOREWORD

There is no shortage of books about Segovia, describing his life and accomplishments, and recording some of his most memorable sayings – a field in which he seems to have rivalled Dr. Samuel Johnson; it is not my object to add to these. What appears in this book stems from my personal contact with him during 39 years of friendship, not from mere journalistic diligence; it contains my experiences and impressions of him, with minimal reference to external sources. He was one of those towering figures in the history of the classic guitar, whose influence was comparable with those of Fernando Sor, Antonio Torres, Francisco Tárrega and Albert Augustine, all of whom radically changed the course of the instrument's history. Segovia's influence on the course of my own life was equally definitive; without it I would probably have ended my working days as they began, as a professional scientist and an amateur musician.

Many people have represented themselves as a 'pupil of Segovia' or as having 'studied with' him, frequently to feed their own self-esteem, or with greater concern with the concomitant publicity value of the assertion than for any real truth it might contain. He regularly said that he never had any pupil except for himself, and he once told me: "All over the world I have 'pupils' I have never met!" Yet in a sense we have, unless we are remarkably dull, *all* been his students and have learned *something* from him. My personal relationship with him was never that of the formal, master/student kind, yet I learned many things from him through observation, questioning and osmosis, as doubtless did many others to whom he extended his friendship. Mine was a minor role in the 'movie' of his life, but his was a major one in that of mine.

I have never kept a diary and my appointments desk-diary survives only as far back as 1973, and only once [1] did I ever tape-record any conversation with Segovia; I never interviewed him formally, though I had innumerable chances to do so. Our meetings were simply those of friends who shared common interests and I never thought of them in any 'archival' way. Many of the things he said were in confidence and would almost certainly not have been said in the presence of an active microphone; I shall try to exclude the most sensitive of those things from this book [1] – but without suppressing anything that affects historical truth, insofar as it contributes to a proper portrayal of Segovia *as I found him to be*. There is a measure of convenience in the chapter headings: the compartmentalization is less clear-cut than they might suggest. One cannot entirely separate the guitarist from the musician, or the man himself from either.

My own view of Segovia inevitably shifted over the years, from one of awestruck adulation to one of greater realism, as he changed from the status of a demigod, viewed from afar, to that of a massively gifted human being, with his due share of weaknesses and foibles, seen at close quarters. Familiarity certainly did not breed contempt. Some time after their deaths, the reputations of most famous men suffer diminution; the carrion take their long-awaited chance to feed on a soft target and, quite properly, the doors of woodsheds are opened by those devoted to establishing historical accuracy, though their revelations may sometimes contribute little more than the fruits of gratuitous '*voyeurism.*' Despite these depredations the reputations of the deserving have a way of being restored, albeit modified by the elimination of misjudgments, misrepresentations and fables. *Pace* The Bard, it is manifestly untrue that it is only man's misdeeds that live on. At the peril of being proved by history to be wrong, I feel safe in predicting that, when the dust has settled, Segovia will retain his place in the guitar's Valhalla. Whatever it was that he did, or did not do, it changed in some way the lives of almost everyone concerned with the classic guitar, whether immediately, indirectly or at long range. It was my good fortune that his path and mine met, and ran parallel so often and over so long a period of time.

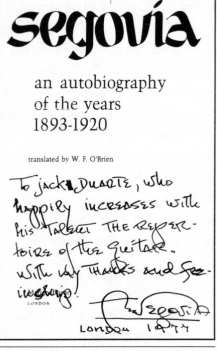

On flyleaf of his autobiography, written at its launch in London: "To Jack Duarte, who happily increases with his talent the repertoire of the guitar. With my thanks and friendship."

PRELUDE

My boyhood ambition was to be a chemist, to which end I entered the Faculty of Technology of Manchester University in 1936, emerging in 1940 with an Honours Degree. As World War II was by then in progress I passed directly into industry as a chemist. Music, in the form of jazz, had entered my life in late 1934, when I began about one and a half years of plectrum-guitar lessons with the late Terence ('Terry') Usher, with whom I remained in close contact until I moved from Manchester to London in 1953. Terry was also interested in the classic guitar and he became increasingly so; it was inevitable that some of his enthusiasm should have rubbed off on to me, and that is how I first encountered Segovia – through those early (1927-1939) 78-r.p.m. records, some of which I still have. At that time I never dreamed that, more than 40 years later, I would write the sleevenotes for their reissue in the LP format [2] and would receive a Grammy Award for doing it! These were magical sounds, but so far removed from anything I was then doing, or visualized being directly concerned with, that they did not prompt me to do more than listen to and enjoy them. However, as a jazz musician and therefore one to whom extemporizing music was a natural way of life, the notion of composing something for the classic guitar did seem realistic – and attractive. My interest in 'classical' music had begun shortly before that and I was already educating myself in its workings via the standard textbooks, so it was not entirely unfamiliar territory. Thus, in the late 1930s I wrote my first, very forgettable pieces, using my right-hand fingers (badly) on my plectrum guitar.

Sometime in the mid-1940s I bought a Panormo guitar from a pawnshop for £5 and sold it a year later for £10, replacing it with a full-size instrument by an obscure Spanish luthier of this century. Whilst I made no detectable effort to acquire a correct right-hand playing position or action, my left-hand facility served me well enough for my immediate purposes. I began to develop a degree of feeling for the particular character of the classic instrument; with it came the urge to write something more substantial for it.

At about the same time, Terry and I founded the Manchester Guitar Circle, most of the pre-1953 meetings of which were held in my home. My fluent sight-reading and rough-and-ready playing technique were put to regular use in helping to fill out the programmes of the meetings, particularly in playing duets with Terry. Sometimes we would play Bach or Handel, for instance, directly from the keyboard scores; I read from the bass clef, which, since I then also played the double-bass, presented no difficulty – and saved time.

There was no debate at that time: a few records of other guitarists crossed our aural horizons but Segovia was by 'divine right' the god at the head of our hexachordal totem pole. The young Julian Bream visited the Circle in the late 1940s, his head appearing above his guitar like Mr. Chad's, but we saw him only as a 'prospect' for the distant future – if all went well, 'the next Segovia?' In those (and later) days the description was freely bestowed upon any young person whose guitaristic prowess approached what we might now rate as about that of Grade Seven (Associated Board). All did go very well for young Bream, but most of the others sank without leaving a ripple on the surface, as so many still do. There was, I think, a latent fear that the classic guitar might die with Segovia, with whom it was then virtually identified, prompting this earnestly ingenuous search for his 'successor.' The situation was encapsulated in an article published at that time (in which journal, I do not remember): "After Segovia, what?" Now he *is* dead and time has answered that question.

The foregoing describes sufficiently well the scenario of my life and musical condition into which Segovia was soon to enter. When he did, his effect on it was, strange as it may seem, neither dramatic nor immediate but, rather, long-range. It did not become determinative until 1969, when I finally turned my back on chemistry and devoted the remainder of my life to music and the guitar.

CHAPTER ONE

Early Encounters
(1948-1952)

Late in 1947 the news reached us that Segovia was to give a recital for the Bradford Music Society, whereupon members of the Manchester Guitar Circle hired a Rolls Royce, which seemed appropriate to the occasion, and were driven in style across the wintry moors to partake of the Ultimate Experience; the Sounds were to reach us without the intervention of gramophone or radio, and their maker was to become incarnate. I now recollect almost nothing of the recital itself, of what or how he played, but the 'coda,' the *après-récital*, remains vividly in my memory. The recital took place in a long room in the Midland Hotel, and in order to reach the platform Segovia had to walk the length of the aisle between the chairs; we were seated nearer to the back than the front of the room and we had no difficulty in accosting him as he passed by in making his final exit. When he learned that we were guitar enthusiasts, even more an organization thereof, he invited us to join him in the lounge, an offer that was reflexively accepted.

Adulatory amateurs dog the footsteps of all great (and many not-so-great) artists, some of whom find it difficult to conceal their boredom and impatience with those who, in the last analysis, provide them with their living, but Segovia was not one of those, nor did he ever become one. Writing in *B.M.G.* magazine (February 1948) I gave our impressions: "Reports from certain sources had represented Segovia to us as an unapproachable and even disagreeable man ... after the recital we spent some time with Segovia and found him to be a most friendly, helpful and charming human being – more than that, he displayed an ease of manner and a gentlemanliness which are all too seldom found in this country today."

The content of the conversation itself, probably for the most part obsequious small-talk, is long-forgotten, but its end is not. Terry was one of a small number of people who changed my life by administering gentle nudges in what they felt to be right directions for me, with greater faith in my potential than I had. I was a professional scientist and a musical hobbyist, and I envisaged no change in that comfortable *status quo*. On this occasion the nudge was an indirect one: Terry had brought with him the manuscript of my most ambitious composition to date, the *Sonata in D minor, Op. 4*,[3] and he passed it to Segovia. The piece was meant to be a homage to Beethoven, one of my idols at the time, but it was far more redolent of Sor, as Segovia may have noticed as he very carefully scrutinised it. Whatever the case, he made sounds of approval and, as we departed into the night, he said to

Terry (talking 'past' me, in the third person): "Keep him working and keep me informed about what he writes." I took this as a gesture of politeness, rather than an expression of serious interest, and did not embark forthwith on any burst of creative effort. Indeed, I wrote only one more small piece in that year.

MANCHESTER: 1948

The second encounter took place sooner than I had expected. Manchester was then, as it still is, the home of the Hallé Orchestra, whose conductor at that time was John Barbirolli (the 'Sir' was added one year later), a devoted admirer of Segovia and the proud possessor of every recording he had made. To the blank astonishment of the orchestra's administrators he instructed them to invite Segovia to play in a Hallé Concert. At that stage the news that man had landed on one of the outer planets would have seemed no more remarkable than the notion that a guitarist might share the platform with the Hallé, or any other distinguished orchestra. However, J.B. was accustomed to getting what he wanted. Segovia duly arrived to play the Castlenuovo-Tedesco Concerto, with a few solos thrown in for good measure.

It was in fact even better than that: the Free Trade Hall, the traditional home of the Hallé Concerts, had been razed to the ground by the airborne minions of an overambitious house painter, one Adolf Hitler, who did not live to tender for the contract when the Hall was rebuilt. The concerts were thus perforce transferred to the Queen's Hall, just across the street; as this was much smaller, each concert, including Segovia's, was repeated on successive evenings. In retrospect it is hard to say truthfully how much we *heard* of the guitar in the Concerto performances, but it was rather more than we had expected. That we heard it *at all* – and *twice,* was enough; it was our first experience of such an exotic thing. The closest one can now come to reliving the experience is through the recording that Segovia made in July 1949 [4]; the orchestra and conductor are different but it gives a fair impression of how Segovia played that work, at that time.

The visit was musically memorable, and it was equally so in another way. The Secretary of the Hallé Society, T.E. Bean (who later became Manager of the Royal Festival Hall in London) had in line of duty to entertain Segovia, and he was a little apprehensive of having to talk at length with a great musician of whose special field he knew next to nothing. Accordingly he invited Terry and I to dine with them at the Constitutional Club in St. Peter's Square. One of the solos Segovia had played was by Villa-Lobos (Study No. 1, I think), and this prompted Bean to tell us that the Hallé Society had received a letter from him, proposing that they should invite him to Manchester to conduct an entire concert of his own music, though not of course the Guitar Concerto, which he had not yet written! The suggestion provoked benevolent amusement, since Villa-Lobos' name was virtually unknown in Britain at that time. Needless to say, the concert never did take place, but it provided a topic of conversation. The evening as a whole was important to Terry and me in establishing a more personal relationship with Segovia than any that might have developed from a green-room encounter after a recital.

MANCHESTER: 1949

The bond was considerably strengthened one year later, when Segovia returned to Manchester, this time to give a solo recital in the Houldsworth Hall (Deansgate), the home of the then-

---

famous Tuesday Midday Concerts – of which Segovia's was not one, on 4 November. Terry and I were delegated to supply the programme notes; they now look embarrassingly amateurish, but we had never before done such a thing! It was a bitterly cold night, that cannot have been helpful to Segovia's hands, and it must be admitted that he was not at the peak of his form. We were somewhat taken aback to find that he was capable of making slips of both memory and fingers, but it did reveal him to us as a human being – and therefore fallible. Somehow it helped to 'normalise' our personal relationship with him.

After the recital, Segovia moved on to a reception given by the Hallé Club; we went home to prepare for our own major event, the arrival of Segovia and his travelling companion, the marvellous Brazilian singer/guitarist Olga Coelho, for dinner. The meal successfully despatched (my wife is a superb cook) we retired to what is known in northern parts as the 'drawing room' to relax. Olga, exhausted by travelling, did so comprehensively by falling asleep on the settee. How, we asked ourselves, could *anyone* fall asleep in the presence of the great You-know-who? Inevitably, Segovia asked what I had written since our previous meeting (the honest answer was 'not much') and suggested that I might play it to him. This was *not* what I had expected! I carefully half-turned in self-defense, so that he would not see the ramshackle workings of my right hand, but the ploy was unsuccessful; he leaned forward until he had a clear view. Having satisfied himself that he was missing nothing he would have wanted to see, he settled back and contented himself with listening to the product. This was in a sense a pivotal moment: he, recognizing that I was an incipient composer who was in no danger of becoming a performer, had accepted that my 'technique' served the sole purpose of giving some impression of the music, the real heart of the matter; instinctively realizing this with much relief, I immediately lost all fear of playing for him – and it never returned. Several times in later years, when we were alone together, he passed his guitar to me, saying: "Play something, Jack"; I invariably did so, without trepidation, choosing pieces (seldom my own) that were easy enough for me to play them musically.

One of my 'exhibits' that evening was to reverberate through the rest of my life. As an academic exercise I had made an arrangement of the *Gigue* from the Third Cello Suite of Bach and, although (maybe *because*!) I did not play it, this greatly interested Segovia. About six years later I treated the remaining movements in similar fashion to produce a Suite that has been recorded 12 times, one of them by Segovia himself. It was not at his suggestion that it was completed, but if his reception of that first experiment had not been encouraging I might not have continued.

Two more lessons were learned that evening. Terry played something from the standard repertory but went astray at one point, upon which Segovia appropriated the guitar and demonstrated how it should have been – after which he continued to play for some time. The first lesson was, then, that if you wanted Segovia to play in an intimate, social situation, it was necessary only to play something he knew, in a way that provoked him to show you the error of your ways. We were quick learners! The other related to his playing. It is not too difficult to imagine how awe-inspiring it then was to hear Segovia playing, within touching distance, in your own home, experiencing the familiar tonal richness and variety at such close quarters. But of course, one thought comfortingly, he had an immense advantage – the best guitar that money could buy, the one you dream of having but never will. The self-deception evaporated at the moment when I realized that *his* guitar was still in its case, in the hallway, and that what he was playing was *my* instrument! There was no longer any place to hide from the truth: the difference lay in the player, rather than the instrument, and those opulent sounds were being coaxed from my cheap, very undistinguished (£15) box. Worse, it carried strings whose youth was a distant memory. I have always been lazy about changing strings, unless one breaks or becomes false; not being a performer, I tend to feel that the necessary time and labour might be better spent on something more relevant to my active musical life. Some years later, again in an at-home situation, he casually picked up my guitar and, after playing a few bars on it, said: "These *strings!*" in a far from enthusiastic tone of voice. I admitted: "Yes, I think they're the same ones that were on when you came last year." He made no further comment.

LONDON: 1950

Segovia did not return to Manchester before 1953, the year in which I left the city where I had lived for most of my life. In 1950, however, Terry and I travelled to London to meet him at his then-usual *pied-à-terre*, the Piccadilly Hotel. This time I showed him a short piece I had recently written, the *Prelude Op. 13/1.* [5] Having inspected it he laid it aside, saying that it is impossible to sight-read on the guitar (a statement that should not be taken at its face value), but retained it. Some time after that he excused himself, saying that he had something else to attend to, but asked us to return an hour or two later. When we did so he played the piece; it was the first time I heard him play anything I had written. During our absence he had obviously devoted time to arriving at a satisfactory fingering. The music met with his approval and he said, that if I would extend the piece and add two more movements, one song-like and the other dance-like, he would play the resulting 'suite.' I was now at least half-convinced that he was genuinely interested and, naturally enough, I wasted no time in setting about the task when I got home. Despite prolonged efforts I was unable to find any satisfactory extension to the *Prelude*; it was complete within its modest 23 bars, and that was that! So the project died on the doorstep, and with it the enviable opportunity – but I had learned another lesson.

SHEFFIELD: 1952

We met only once more during my sojourn in Manchester. In 1952 he played a recital in the Cutlers' Hall in Sheffield and, together with friends, I went to hear it. After the recital we went to a small reception at the home of a local *aficionado*, where Segovia was regaled with a performance of my *Sonatina Op. 15* [6] for flute and guitar, in which I was partnered by Joan Mitchell, a young lady whose abundant musical talents included some skill with the flute. There was no prospect that Segovia might take any direct interest in the piece, for he played little in the way of chamber music and, to the best of my knowledge, never played in duo with a flautist; it was simply a matter of keeping him *au fait* with my output. Joan was a far better player that I was, but, unaware of the benevolence of his personality – especially when confronted with a personable young lady, I believe she was the more nervous in his presence!

Had I continued to live in Manchester, a city to which he rarely came, my contact with Segovia would have been far more tenuous and the course of my life would almost certainly have been very different. This small book would never have been written.

CHAPTER TWO

Development
(1953-1987)

Although my contact with Segovia was minimal in 1952 it was nevertheless a crucial year for me. Terry and I had known a guitarist called Len Williams in the mid-1930s, before Neville Chamberlain's assurance that is was to be "peace in our time" had prompted that politically aware gentleman to emigrate to Australia. Now he had returned to London, accompanied by his wife (Melaan), son (John Christopher) and sundry antipodean acolytes, where he established the first Spanish Guitar Centre in Britain. In his professional capacity as Public Relations Officer to Manchester Corporation, Terry made periodic visits to London to attend meetings of the National Association of Local Government

Officers (NALGO), and in October 1952 I went with him on one of these forays with the object of re-meeting Len Williams – and witnessing the remarkable talent of his 11-year-old son. Over several pints of ale in the local pub, Len (and his supporting cast) persuaded me to move to London in order to teach John, which I did from 1953 until the time (1956) when he entered the Royal College of Music. Thus, in March 1953 the Duartes migrated southward. I took a post as Chief Chemist with a small company in Stoke Newington and we bought a house in Southgate, about one mile from the Williams' home in Bounds Green. The change of location strengthened my links with Segovia; I now lived in the one city in Britain to which he came once or twice each year. The keyword was propinquity – and it soon turned in the lock.

Segovia returned in the early winter of the same year and visited us in our new home, again in the company of Olga Coelho, who gave an unforgettable recital in the Wigmore Hall on 3 November – almost exactly four years after our first meeting. Segovia was in the audience, seated next to the artist Annigoni, then famous for his portrait of the Queen. I have long lost count of the record sleevenotes I have written, but the first was for a recording by Olga (a long-deleted EP on the Starlite label), an assignment stemming from a later visit by her and Segovia in the mid-1950s. It was also in 1953 that Segovia first met John Williams, at our home.

Thereafter we met on countless occasions, at home or at his hotel, either for a meal or a passing visit, or occasionally in other people's homes. It soon became clear that he enjoyed his visits to us as opportunities to relax, often taking off his coat and shoes and putting his feet up – in which semi-supine attitude he sometimes played my guitar. We thus avoided turning his visits into

Chapter Two

'peepshows' by filling the house with warm but minimally con-
tributive bodies, creating the kind of situation we had seen elsewhere, in which he felt obliged to entertain an assembled company that had little idea of how to entertain *him* in a relaxed way,
usually drawing on his rich fund of anecdotes. The largest gathering we ever assembled was on one evening in the earlyish 1960s,
when both Segovia and Alirio Diaz came to dinner and we were
later joined by John Williams and Michael Watson, the founder of
the Spanish Guitar Centre in Bristol. The guitar (whose, I forget)
circulated amongst three famous pairs of hands; mine (*not* famous!) were occupied only in refreshing drinks and refilling
my pipe.

On many of his visits to London Segovia travelled alone, and
at such times he often telephoned to me at various times of day or
evening, sometimes just to say 'Hello' or to outline some project
he had in mind, but more often to ask if I could join him in his
hotel room – he just wanted company. Occasionally we would
take a walk in the West End (he particularly liked the shops in
Bond Street and, as he was a collector of silverware, those in the
Burlington Arcade) and often we would head for Dunhill's shop in
Duke Street to replenish his stock of his special mixture of pipe
tobacco. At the same time he would usually buy a separate quan-
tity for me; I was never so ungracious as to tell him that such a
light and aromatic mixture was not really to my taste! As so many
pictures testify, Segovia was a contented pipe-smoker, but in his
autumnal years he was weaned away from it by his last wife,
Emilita, who guarded his equipment (and health!) and, when
asked, filled his pipe – more sparingly than I had previously seen
him to do!

OF SHIPS AND STRING AND SEALING-WAX

At his hotel we talked of many things, not always music-related. On one occasion he casually asked me (a veritable *non sequitur*) if there was any upper limit on the age at which one could hold a British driving licence. A call to Savile Row police station confirmed that there was none. He then proceeded to unfold his characteristically complex plan. He drove a good deal in Spain, where he had by then returned to live, but there was a small problem: one could not apply for the renewal of one's driving licence after one's seventieth birthday, an occasion on which he then looked back from some distance. The problem was an ethical rather than practical one: if the Spanish police asked to see his driving licence he had none to show, but when they learned who he was they would deferentially wave him on his way without further ado. This did not sit comfortably on his conscience. The plan was, therefore, that he would take up residence in London for as long as it took him to obtain a British driving licence, with which he could automatically get an International Driving Permit – which was valid in Spain! On his next visit he was accompanied by Emilita, and during a conversation in his room at the Westbury Hotel I mentioned that I was going from there to a recital by Alirio Diaz at the Wigmore Hall; they had not known of this and said they would like to go with me, so I drove them there. As we dismounted I asked Segovia how his driving-licence plan was progressing but, with his back half-turned at that moment, he did not hear me. Before I could repeat the question Emilita touched my arm, put her finger to her lips, shook her head and whispered: "His eyes!" So perished another project – but this one was *his*.

While on the subject of motoring in our previous conversation, Segovia had recalled a time between the two World Wars when, having collected a splendid new car in the south of France, he was driving it back to Paris. He came up behind a small, dilapidated car which repeatedly frustrated his attempts to overtake it by lurching into the centre of the road. Eventually they came to a hill, the ascent of which absorbed the entire energy of the offending vehicle, depriving it of the capacity to lurch sideways. Segovia drew level with it, lowered his window and tersely vented his feelings on the other driver: *"Idiot! Crétin! Imbécile!"* The response was: "Andrés!"; answered by: "Pablo!" They pulled into the roadside, Segovia and Picasso. The former asked what the latter was doing in such a deplorable disaster on wheels, and was told that it had been given to him that morning in settlement of a small debt. It being established that Picasso also hoped to reach Paris, and didn't really want what he was driving, they continued their journey in Segovia's car, leaving the tired old veteran by the wayside – to be salvaged by someone who would know nothing of its briefly distinguished history! We all have our brushes on the highways and byways, but in our cases the other driver is more likely to be Joe Bloggs. Throwaway anecdotes such as this are by-products of longer and richer lives than are given to most of us.

The Spanish Civil War had driven Segovia, a devoted royalist, into exile. He had to depart hastily, taking only what he could carry, and leaving, *inter alia*, many irreplaceable music manuscripts – one of the several heavy losses he sustained during his long life. By the time he felt it safe to return, in the easier climate of the early 1950s, all his abandoned possessions had been dispersed and lost. Having resumed his Spanish citizenship he decided to build a house in the depths of his beloved Granada, a little place to which he could retreat, especially during the summer months. He bought a plot of land in Almuñecar, overlooking the sea, and asked an architect friend to draw up the plans according to the layout he visualized. The plans were approved and work began. There came, however, periodical requests for advance funds, to deliver which and to monitor the progress of the work Emilita visited the site, often leaving Segovia to travel alone in the 1960s. It gradually became apparent that something was amiss: the building was taking its expected shape, but it was far larger than they had anticipated. Segovia's many talents did not include that of reading architectural plans accurately; the layout was one thing but the scale was another! What was rising from the earth's surface was more like a national monument than a cozy little nest in the country – but what had been started had to be finished. One day when we were together we added up the estimated final cost of the enterprise: I will say only that it was very considerable, and much greater than he had anticipated. However he consoled himself pragmatically with the view, that it would be an investment for the future, especially Emilita's after his death. That house, "Los Olivos," is now 'known' to many watchers of television documentaries – and I am sure that Segovia never regretted having sanctioned it, even though unwittingly! When it was completed he said annually to my wife and me: "You must come immediately to Spain, to visit my new home." Our distaste for the Franco régime was, however, so strong that we just as regularly declined; when the situation had changed the time had somehow passed – we never did go there.

LANGUAGES

Segovia had an excellent command of several languages, notably French, Italian and English; when I asked him if he spoke German he said: "Only in self-defense!" Whilst his English grammar and syntax were often quaint, and one could easily detect those points at which his English was 'translated Spanish,' his meaning was always clear. He frequently used uncommon words that would not feature in the everyday speech of the average Englishman, but he never misused one; such words were always precisely correct in their context. Though they did not contain any verbal exotica, two phrases, occurring mainly in telephone conversations, stick fondly in the memory: "Telephone to me tomorrow at ten o'clock; we will combine something together" (translated Spanish) and "I send many things to your wife."

My few attempts to speak with him in French were less than successful. I had learned the language at school, whereas he may have acquired it through practical use, and we spoke it with very different accents. Whilst neither of us had any real problem in speaking to French people, we did so when talking to one another. One whose native language is 'Y' can readily 'translate' the pronunciations of others whose mother tongues are, say, 'X' and 'Z,' but the distance between 'X' and 'Z' is greater, not least when 'Y' is not the *langue maternelle* of either! Segovia's French, though fluent, lacked·the nasal sounds of true French; for instance, he pronounced the first syllable of *'maintenant'* as an Englishman would say 'main.' Like many others whose native tongue is of Latin derivation, he assumed that the name 'Jack,' by which I was known to family and friends, was spelt 'Jacques' – which of course means 'James,' not 'John.' [7] The belief was naturally reinforced by my surname, common in 'Latin' countries, but my father was a Scot and my mother was English! After he had understood the difference I could often tell from his letters those times when he was in a disturbed or depressed state of mind; at such times the envelope was usually addressed to 'Jacques Duarte.' One envelope was so designated in the late summer of 1968, not too long after the tragic and totally unexpected death of his daughter, Beatriz, at the age of twenty-nine; she had been the apple of his eye. The letter ended: "And now I must return to work, but it is without enthusiasm."

This has so far been a broad account of the nature and 'flavour' of my contacts with Segovia. The remaining chapters will constitute a more detailed description and assessment of his work and character as they appeared to me.

Andrés Segovia with John Duarte's wife Dorothy at the launch of the first part of Segovia's autobiography at the Spanish Institute in London (1977). Dorothy is holding Segovia's glass! (Photo: Maurice Summerfield, courtesy *Classical Guitar Magazine*)

CHAPTER THREE

Segovia
the musician

During Segovia's formative years musical Romanticism was
flourishing, nowhere more strongly than in Spain, where there was
a late flowering in the form of a 'new wave' school of compositional nationalism, triggered by the teachings of Felipe Pedrell and
aimed at throwing off the chronic domination of Spanish music by
Italian tastes and practices. It was spearheaded by Turina,
Granados, Albéniz and Falla, all of whose lives overlapped with
Segovia's: the first to die was Albéniz, in 1909 (the year of
Segovia's debut recital) and the last was Turina, in 1949; thus, to
Segovia, what they were writing was *contemporary* music. Romanticism was enthusiastically embraced in Spain and it found a
concomitant resonance in Segovia's temperament, one to which
he remained faithful to the end of his life. In this music he found
reflections of the beauty of the countryside, architecture, poetry

and plastic arts of Spain, constituting an idealized dream-world in which, artistically, he was enviably content to dwell; he was well aware of the harsher side of life's coin but he wanted no more part of it than he was obliged to experience – and for him it certainly had no place in music. Idealism, focused on music and the guitar, was a major driving force in his life.

Love and passionate belief are important factors in healthy idealism and they certainly were so in Segovia's brand of it. One day when we were alone he asked me what I had been working on recently: I told him I had just finished arranging guitar accompaniments to several songs of Schubert, so he asked which ones I had done. The first one I named was *Du bist die Ruh'* (Thou art my peace) and, to my surprise, he sang through the melody in solfeggio. As Schubert wrote many hundreds of songs, many of which were far better known than this one, it seemed to me a remarkable feat of memory – and I said so. His response was: "When music *moves* me I *always* remember it." The keyword was 'moves': I do not believe that he ever played even one small piece that he did not love or believe in, or which did not in some way move him.

Like all true musicians, Segovia recognized that, in delivering a naturally phrased musical line, the human voice was the supreme instrument. When making a musical point, whether in private or in a master class, he would often sing the phrase in solfeggio as well as, or instead of, playing it on the guitar; one instance of this is unlikely to fade from my memory. We had walked to his favorite Spanish restaurant, just off Regent Street, where, since it was still early in the evening, we found only a handful of people at the tables. The majordomo greeted Segovia in a manner befitting 'royalty' and asked us to wait for a moment.

Two people were dining at the table where Segovia usually sat; they were, despite his protestation that it did not matter, politely but firmly moved, lock stock and cutlery, to another table. Being unused to such benefit of status I felt less than comfortable – but worse was to come! By that time I had completed the arrangement of the Third Cello Suite of Bach, of which Segovia had seen only the *Gigue* in 1949. He had heard the whole Suite earlier that year, played by John Williams in Siena, so I asked his opinion of it: "It is very good – but the *Bourrées* go too high on the fingerboard." So I pointed out to him that they went no further than the *Courante*, which he himself had arranged – and not as far as Tárrega's inappropriately harmonized arrangement, which he had recorded! He responded by singing the offending *galanteries* through, from beginning to end – and quite loudly. I wished for a cloak of invisibility but none materialized; a 'Latinate,' less reserved temperament would have made a good substitute, but I am irretrievably 'English'! Having delivered himself of the last note, he said: "You are right." There the matter rested until, some years later, he recorded the Suite, *Bourrées* and all. [8]

He frequently said that a performer should always be at the service of his composers, respecting the identity of each, yet he was one of those *Grands Artistes* who, like Kreisler, Ysäe and Rachmaninov, for instance, was always immediately recognizable by his sound and his interpretative approach. Hearing him play on record or on the radio one first thought: "That's Segovia playing" and *then*, "The composer is..." He would almost certainly have been offended by the suggestion that he imprinted his own personality on that of every composer he played, but that is exactly how it was. A composer was as he perceived him to be, as a facet of his own musical personality, rather than as our knowledge of history revealed him. There is an element of this in the playing of many great artists, but in Segovia's case it was very strong. Such, however, was the force and integrity of his own convictions that he was regarded, even by many academically informed musicians, as one of the great interpreters of our times. He had a near-miraculous ability to bring about the willing suspension of disbelief in listeners who, if anyone else had approached, say, pre-classical music in a comparable way, would have risen in arms, uttering loud protestations of 'anachronism and misrepresentation.' This may well have been due in some measure to the sheer amazement, on the part of musicians who knew little or nothing of the guitar that was to its advantage, that this humble instrument could be persuaded to reveal contrapuntal lines with such clarity, but both critics and musicians (even those who merit *both* descriptions) have continued to comment on this, despite the prevailing, much more acute awareness of, and respect for period style. Segovia was in many ways a law unto himself, a king who could do no wrong in the ears of his many subjects, a magician who wove spells over his audiences, unmeasured by the criteria that applied to most others.

ATTITUDE TO PRE-CLASSICAL MUSIC

Beyond reasonable doubt, Segovia loved what is loosely described as 'early' music, a term that owes more to familiarity than to precise definability [9]; in it he found a dignified expression of the gamut of human emotion (that is to say, the good aspects thereof) in wholly tonal language and through lucid structures. Whilst he naturally held the *vihuelistas* in special affection, he had a profound love of the music of many 'non-Spanish' composers, of whom Dowland, de Visée, Scarlatti, Handel and, especially, Bach (in whose music he perceived the apotheosis of the reconciliation of expressive beauty with intellectual mastery), were but a few. It was not just the complexity and apparently mathematical precision of a fugue which appealed to him, it was the miraculous way in which these things were so naturally brought to the service of emotion – from sombre dignity to gaiety.

In order to understand Segovia's approach to early music we must look back at least one century before the year of his birth. Public, pay-at-the-door concerts, the main platform for presenting art music to a wide cross-section of the populace, were basically devoted to then-contemporary music. What had been written in earlier times was past history, of which composers were aware – Beethoven, for instance, possessed and revered scores of some of Bach's works, but the public was little concerned with it. During the nineteenth century there developed an increasing awareness of earlier musics, fostered by a number of people, of whom Mendelssohn is best-remembered for his advocacy of Bach's music. Mixed programmes of contemporary and earlier musics became more common, not least after the foundation of the Henry Wood Promenade Concerts in London. This was reflected in the activities of guitarists: the recitals of Sor, Giuliani *et al* had been based on their own music, and reworkings of other men's music were centered on their contemporaries, e.g., Giuliani's cap-touchings to Rossini, but Tárrega arranged music by Mozart, Bach, Handel, Beethoven, Chopin and others whose deaths had predated his own birth. By this time, early music had become 'fashionable,' even a badge of cultural status, so Tárrega composed pieces with 'early-music' titles – *Minueto, Gavota* and *Pavana*, though their connection with those earlier dances was at best tenuous.

All this was nevertheless only a beginning; the resuscitation of early music had (maybe still has) a long road to travel. Proper awareness of matters such as accuracy of text, the role of period instruments, playing techniques and, above all, performance styles had yet to emerge beyond the confines of 'rarefied' academia – within which there was then far less information available than there is today. A certain amount of knowledge existed, and was even put into practice, but little happened publicly before 1900. That great pioneer in the field Arnold Dolmetsch (1858-1940) first performed in public in 1890 and for much of his life was regarded by the music-world at large as an enlightened (but eccentric) academic. The harpsichordist Wanda Landowska (1879-1959) did not play her instrument in public until 1903. Although many great performers must have been aware of the work of these and other distinguished 'revivalists' it did not noticeably touch their daily lives and work. They began to play the solo, chamber and larger works of, for instance, Bach, but very much in the style to which they were accustomed – essentially romantic. The notes of these early works had been written in other ages, but musical expression had by then acquired romantic coloration – and the 'then' was an age (Victorian/Edwardian) that was full of self-confidence, one towards which (it was believed) earlier ages had evolved. To all but the most informed (and caring), there was absolutely nothing wrong in playing, say, baroque music in a manner not far removed from that in which one would properly play one's own 'contemporary' music. Trills, for instance, had by then become 'antipodean,' commencing with the main note, and it was half a century before musicians of most kinds learned that a baroque trill is the 'other way up' – and acted on it; some still have not!

'Authentic' performances of early music were fairly widespread between, say, the 1920s and the 1940s but they came mostly from specialists, with whose 'academic' doings the 'general-purpose' virtuoso had little to do. Widespread concern with proper period practices is a comparatively recent phenomenon, dating roughly from the 1950s and catalyzed in England by the performing, research and teaching skills of Robert Thurston Dart (1921-1971).

If I have dwelt on this subject at comparative length it is in order to give some idea of the state of matters relating to early music and its performance at the time of Segovia's arrival and 'formation,' and for the first four or five decades of his active career. He lacked a formal academic education in music, but, at the time when he might have enjoyed one, it would probably have done little to enhance his understanding of the inner core and finer details of pre-classical music, not least since he would have received his education in Spain, where concern with such matters developed even later than it did elsewhere. It is true that Emilio Pujol (1886-1980) was an early leader in the Spanish field, a scholarly researcher and champion of pre-classical music, but he was only seven years older than Segovia, not old enough to be regarded by him as a 'guru' – but, as a near-contemporary who was also embarking on a performing career, he was a potential 'rival.' To what extent Segovia benefited by Pujol's work, particularly that of transcribing tablatures, it is difficult to say. Despite the fact that we often discussed the music of the lutenists and *vihuelistas*, I never ascertained how much of their music Segovia *himself* had transcribed (rather than using someone else's transcription as his source material) – nor, for that matter, whether he was familiar enough with the various forms of tablature to have worked freely from them. Pujol on one side, it is difficult to suggest from whom in Spain he might have acquired special knowledge of early music, even had he felt motivated to do so.

Segovia was born and educated, and 'evolved' musically in Spain, where the art-musical climate was romantic; it resonated with his own nature and shaped his approach to all music – so completely that it remained essentially unchanged throughout his life. He was, too, born in an age when the 'historical,' 'cross-sectional' recital programme was in vogue (and since when it has never been entirely *out* of fashion), and this too suited his purpose admirably: it enabled him to demonstrate that the guitar was capable of presenting music of *all* periods, not just that which was contemporary in his own time. Early music was thus only a part of his (and others') programmes, something which, following Tárrega's lead, he inducted – by whatever means were available, to serve a practical-ideological purpose, and because he was attracted to it – as *music*. By the time the work of the Dolmetsches and others had begun to bear modest fruit Segovia was in his late thirties, and when early-music scholarship truly 'went public' he was approaching sixty. If he did not profit from these advances the same might be said of the great majority of his other-instrumental peers, the pianists, violinists and cellists, who played Bach, for example, in very much the same way at the same time. In their performances they committed similar stylistic peccadillos, though not always in the same *degree* as Segovia, e.g., in applying rubato; the differences were however those among shades of grey, rather than of black *versus* white. Great soloists on *any* instrument tended to live in their own mini-universes and, not least when their careers were flourishing and their days were devoted to maintaining them, they rarely had the time or, perhaps, the motivation, to change horses in mid-stream, radically modifying the way they played the music of a particular period, only a segment of their total working repertoire. They were also, by definition, less free to spend a great deal of time in listening to others, or to embark on re-educating themselves, than the less successful; this was even more the case in the first half of this century, before the record industry grew to its present dimensions and prosperity, making it possible to listen to all kinds of music, anywhere and at any time. Acoustic recording dates back to 1877 but it was not until 1923 that there were sufficient 'consumers' to prompt the first publication of *Gramophone* magazine; long-playing records arrived only in the late 1940s and cassette recorders came about 20 years after that. All of this applied with even greater force to guitarists, including Segovia, whose main activity was to play solo recitals, coming into contact with other musicians only peripherally and rarely playing together *with* them; only now is this situation beginning to change to any worthwhile degree. It would, if anything, have been remarkable if Segovia *had* been significantly touched by early-musicological research, at a time when its impact on his peers was minimal.

THE LUTE

One thing is absolutely clear: Segovia detested the lute! After listening to a tape-recording of the Guitar Concerto of Malcolm Arnold (I was present at the time), which was not to his taste, he said: "It is a pity it was not written for the lute – then it could have discredited the lute instead of the guitar!" What is interesting is not that he disliked the lute, a noble instrument with a golden history and a pleasing sound – however, *di gustibus non est disputandum*, but why he did so – and with such a passion. We can never know with certainty, but my own theory is that the seeds were planted early in his career. Let us try, notionally, to re-enter his mind in those early years, devoted to propagating the classic guitar in a world that was barely aware of its very existence and, for the most part, unlikely to know the difference between a guitar and any other fretted instrument. In order to do this, pre-classical (*viz.* pre-classic-guitar) music is needed for the repertory, and this is available as music written for earlier instruments of the type. However, we do not want to regress by exhuming the four- and five-course, historical instruments, mere steps along the evolutionary path leading to the perfection of the classic guitar, so we gently use adaptations of the music written for them. Nor, heaven forfend, do we want to trigger off a revival of the lute! In this case I think we may reject any impish notion that Segovia was antagonistic to the lute because of its Moorish origins, for he loved the Spanish architecture of that ilk, though we may note that his scorn was never directed against the (Spanish) *vihuela* – but there was then no reason to fear that it might be revived!

The magnificent inheritance of lute music is highly desirable for the expansion of the guitar's repertory, but the lute *per se* needs to be kept in its museum showcase; therefore, let us be at pains to point out what a poor instrument it is, and that the guitar is admirably (and far better) suited to the music that was written for it! What the lute could do, the guitar could do better. We now know very well that this is not the case; a great deal of lute music is not even playable on the guitar without distortion, and some is quite unmanageable. Ironically, the lute has made a strong comeback and is now re-established as a 'standard' early-musical instrument in its own right; this has been achieved without apparent detriment to the guitar. The overall revival of pre-classical music carried the lute with it and was something that was beyond the control or influence of Segovia, or any other guitarist. In all this we have the benefit of hindsight, which Segovia could not have had. It remains speculation and if Segovia did indeed ever pursue such a line of thought, it may well have been subconsciously; however, it does seem to accord with the attitude displayed in many of his statements:

1) I once asked him why the third string of the guitar should not be tuned to F♯ in order to retain the pitch-spacing of lute (or vihuela!) tuning, which in turn affects the left-hand fingering and, often, the capacity to sustain notes for their proper durations. He said: "Because a musician expects to find G on that string, not F♯." Questions such as: "Then what does a *musician* expect to find on the sixth string – E or D? And on the fifth – A or G?" and "Can the Sonata of Castelnuovo-Tedesco, which calls for various *scordature*, not be comfortably played by a musician?" remained unasked; I could recognize an *impasse* when confronted with one.

2) In his last decade he expressed the view that, whilst it is "possible" to retune the third string to F♯ in playing lute music, he preferred to keep it at G and to re-finger the music. The truth is that Segovia played and/or recorded relatively little lute (or even *vihuela*) music, and in very little of what he did play was the tuning of the third string a matter of vital importance. His attitude did however seem to soften in his last years, and this too is in line with the above speculation: by this time the 'battle' was won, the guitar had achieved ubiquitous success despite the rise of the lute, so vehement opposition no longer served any useful purpose – a limited 'retreat' to a reasonable position could be made with dignity and without harm to the guitar.

3) After dinner, one evening in October 1972 when Segovia was at my home, I arranged for my Swedish student Cecilia Peijel to play for him. She had just devoted a whole year to restructuring her technique and was thus understandably nervous. Nevertheless I told her, before the event: "You will begin with Dowland's *Sir*

John Smith, his *Almain*, your third string will be at F♯ and you
will have a capo at the third fret. He will probably say something
awful about it but you won't let it worry you, because we know it
is right." She did indeed begin that way and when she had played
it, very well, he paused, looked over the top of his spectacles and
said: "My dear, that was very nice. It must sound even better on
an *adult* guitar." This was milder than she had expected, so she
kept calm. At the end she won his lavish praise for her musicality
and technique; there was no further mention of her 'transgres-
sions,' and when he returned to London he frequently inquired as
to her progress.

4) He consistently expressed his disapproval of guitars with more
than six strings (tuned in the 'approved' fashions!) and considered
the standard number to be sufficient for any reasonable musical
purpose. I do not know how he reacted to the advocacy of the
eight-string guitar by his favorite protégé José Tomas! I have long
been a strong supporter of the multi-string guitars made by the
late Georg Bolin of Stockholm as vehicles for the lute repertory –
ideal for guitarists who do not want to face the technical problems
of playing the lute itself. One of these, an 11-string *altgitarr* (alto
guitar), tuned to G instead of E, has been in my possession since
1975. On one evening (ca. 1976) after dinner at my home, I decided
to show it to Segovia. I played one short piece to him; he made no
comment, so I played another, with the same result. After four
pieces I decided to call it a day and put the guitar aside, awaiting
the verbal *Blitzkrieg* that seemed inevitable. "It *looks* beautiful
and it *sounds* beautiful" was not what I had expected, but it was
what he said. As it was not his habit to regale me with velvet-
gloved platitudes, I took this as further evidence of the late soften-
ing of his attitude. He had finally confronted most of the charac-

teristics of the lute (though not its double courses) – multiple strings, altered third-string tuning, and higher pitch, without feeling the need to be scathing or dismissive. The classic guitar no longer needed 'protection' of that kind.

TEXTS

During the first decades of Segovia's career, guitarists were decidedly cavalier in many aspects of their treatment of early music. Their principal objective seemed to be that of inducting items of such music into the repertory, but in a way that verged on the autocratic:

1) Proper identification was more often than not lacking, and bald titles such as: '*Sonata* (Scarlatti),' '*Bourrée* (Bach)' and '*Sarabande* (Handel)' were commonly applied. Where keys were given, especially those of Scarlatti sonatas, they were those of the guitar arrangements, not of the original works. The day was still distant when a guitarist would have learned to expect a 'K,' 'BWV' or any other reference to be attached, or even to be told clearly which one of the many pieces bearing a general title (let alone in what original key), by a particular composer, he/she was looking at.

2) Equally uncommon was any declaration of the source of the text from which the arranger had worked. Had the arranger started from the composer's autograph manuscript, from a first edition (if any), from a later one (maybe a piano edition of a harpsichord work), or from another guitar arrangement? It was almost invariably echo that answered.

3) Whatever the 'original,' what radical (if any) changes had the arranger made to the text? Again, echo answered. In cases where the original manuscript (as a photocopy or a facsimile edition) is

readily available there is now no need to specify alterations and/or amendments; interested parties can check for themselves. At that time, however, the vast majority of guitarists (and, for that matter, other ordinary musicians) were unaware of even the limited access to original or dependable sources that then existed; today we are much more fortunate.

4) In the case of early music, not least that originally written in tablature, one might expect the arranger to translate it as accurately as possible, without the exercise of his/her own imagination or 'taste.' Such was not the case; even the scholarly Emilio Pujol was not above making his own, unannounced contributions, *e.g.*, in the well-known *Pavanas* of Gaspar Sanz.

This was the state of play both before and during the years in which Segovia made his many contributions to Schott's Guitar Archives. Neither he nor, perhaps, the other outstanding players who were doing likewise would have foreseen the day when rank-and-file guitarists would be able, and – even more to the point – probably also disposed, to check arrangements against original sources. On the whole, players were just grateful to receive new and high-class repertory from distinguished hands; awareness and expectations of academic niceties, even accuracy, were blissfully low. Questions were seldom asked. There were editors who worked to sound standards, particularly in making *Urtext* editions available, but: (i) these were of nineteenth-century, not earlier music; and (ii) as they were not famous performers their 'profiles' were much lower and they carried less weight. The fact that an edition enshrined the work of a famous virtuoso gave it status and carried the implication that it had thereby been vetted, corrected and even 'improved.' Such was of course often not the case. It is unlikely that Segovia possessed the academic know-how necessary to do this, for he had had no formal musical education – and his self-instruction is equally unlikely to have embraced much of musicology. One example will suffice to bear out this conclusion.

A *Romanesca* of Alonso Mudarra appears in Segovia's edition (Schott GA. 159) and its final bars are revelatory. Whether it was Segovia, or someone else, who made the first transcription from the original tablature, we do not know, but, as it was Segovia who 'endorsed' the end-product by publishing it, this is not of first importance; nor does it matter overly that the sixth string is lowered to D, which it certainly was not in the original. In Ex. 1 I give the final three bars as they are printed in the tablature: Ex. 2 shows the literal transcription of the same passage into staff-notation, and Ex. 3 is the printed 'solution.' (Page 42)

On the first beat of bar two we have a high C♯ above a G, a compound tritone between two voices, which, to say the least, sounds strange in this context; no matter who arrived at this translation, they should have raised a deeply enquiring eyebrow at the very sound of it! Segovia has accepted it as a skeletal form of the dominant seventh chord, in its third inversion, adding A and E, but this too would have been a remarkable phenomenon in music of this period. However, it was accepted. The matter did not rest there, though: (i) the leap of a major third to the C♯ from the preceding A in the same voice still sounds oddly 'one-legged,' so a B has been added to bridge it – but it is someone else's, not Mudarra's; (ii) the F below the aforesaid A is natural but, as there is an F♯ in the upper voice, two beats earlier, making a familiar false relation: this is 'tidied up' by being converted to another F♯; (iii) the D that follows the C♯ looks and sounds very odd – it seems to follow the C♯, but in the wrong octave; thus it is transferred to this higher octave and given full, second-inversion, tonic harmony, the logical resolution of the previous chord.

The resulting text, arrived at by radical surgery, could scarcely convince anyone who understood this type and period of music in any depth; it is the consequence of approaching the passage as though it had been written at least one century later. It also bespeaks a touching but misplaced faith in the infallibility of tablatures, an assumption that Spanish renaissance (if no other) printers just didn't make mistakes! Wrong again! The troublesome C♯ corresponds to a figure '9' in the tablature – but suppose the typesetter put in a '6,' upside down – all too easy to do, what then? Ex. 4 shows the same bars, assuming this mistake to have been made, with the '9' changed to a '6.' (i) The note above the G is now a perfectly believable B♭, (ii) the awkward-sounding leap from A to C♯ disappears, and (iii) the 'wrong-octave' D now takes its proper place as an inner voice, completing a chord of G minor (IV). The whole passage finally makes sense. What this indicates, clearly enough, is that the transcriber of the tablature was not really attuned to the sounds and language of the music in question; if he was not that person, Segovia could have asked questions instead of imposing anachronism on the music, or at least sanctioning it. The whole process is one of first basing a theory on a remarkably dubious 'fact,' and then distorting the surrounding 'evidence' to fit it. From where Segovia then sat, it would not have appeared this way; both he and it were 'victims' of their time, and we should not think too harshly – underinformation, not arrogance or sinister intent, was responsible.

There was a degree of ambivalence in Segovia's attitude towards textual accuracy, and even stylistic fitness. Although he totally accepted my version of the Third Cello Suite of Bach, his reception of that of the First Suite was mixed. The basic problem was that he already played the *Prelude* in Manuel Ponce's version, one I did not like because of its gratuitously added voices, producing harmonies that were not implied in the original score. I mentioned this, only to be told: "But, Jack, it is *beautiful!*" Beautiful, maybe, but Bach it was not. I also questioned the extension of the final, chromatically rising thirds into full diminished seventh chords, but: "But we are in the *twentieth* century, not the eighteenth!" True – but irrelevant! He played and recorded some movements of this Suite, though never the whole, but the Prelude stayed in Ponce's arrangement whilst the others were in mine. I heard him play this selection in early 1974 in the Avery Fisher Hall (New York) and I remain as intrigued as I then was to read in the programme, that the *Prelude* was "arranged by Ponce," whilst the remaining movements were in "Mr Duarte's arrangement." The sleeve of the Spanish RCA recording [10] omits Ponce's name, but the *Prelude* is certainly in his arrangement.

I believe that in later years, when textual fidelity was openly declared to be a *sine qua non*, he became more conscious of it as an area in which adverse criticism might be levelled – against which a convincing defense would, in an academically aware world, be impossible to muster. When I showed him arrangements, especially of baroque music, he would ask whether I had gone back to reliable sources in order to make them; but I knew him for more than 20 years before he asked such a question!

STYLE

There were undoubtedly features in Segovia's performances of pre-classical music that were, as historical evidence informs us, anachronistic: the very free use of rubato (borrowing without repaying, so that the piece becomes longer than it should), the prolonged *rallentandi* on approaching the ends of movements or sections thereof, the liberal use of tone-coloration – often applied with great charm, sometimes illogically, the 'inverted' ornaments, and the dwelling on 'pretty' notes that should not always have been so treated. Yet his way of doing it captivated musicians and others of most kinds, probably because it was done with love and utter conviction. He perceived it as beautiful, but, without the benefit of the stylistic knowledge we now have, treated it in much the same way as the romantic music that was such an important part of his formation. In this he differed only in degree from his other-instrumental counterparts. There was liberal romanticism in the playing of even the devotedly scholarly Wanda Landowska, of whom present-day harpsichordists say: "She was a genius, she was marvellous – but of course we wouldn't do it that way now." I believe that we should now say the same of Segovia.

The manner of performing early music constantly changes and it is to some extent influenced by the prevailing *Zeitgeist*. Romanticism is returning to favor in music at large, a predictable reaction against dry intellectualism, and there is also more expressive freedom in the way early music is played (reaction to the rigid adherence to the 'rules' at all costs; first the letter of the Law, *then* the music – if you're lucky!), but of course the wheel never quite turns full-circle. In the meantime we have acquired more scholarship and we have had the time to absorb certain guidelines into our bloodstream. A measure of 'romantic' freedom *will* return to early-music performance, indeed it is already doing so, but we neither can nor ever should return to Segovia's pre-war variety of it. As a result of what we have learned and absorbed, it is changed – and it can never again be quite the same. It is unlikely that there will ever be a definitive 'end of the line' in our efforts to reconstruct baroque or renaissance performance style and practices faithfully; what we perceive as correct at any one stage depends on what musicological research has told us thus far, and on the air over music at that time – the balance between head and heart. Segovia's way of playing pre-classical musics now sounds quaint to us (as ours may very likely do to future generations) but it would be misguided and arrogant to dismiss it as an idiosyncratic nonsense; he burned with love and respect for this music, and played it with total conviction – as well as his state of informativeness allowed. His recording of the *Chaconne* of Bach remains a thing of majesty, even though there are others that display greater stylistic fidelity.

ATTITUDE TO CONTEMPORARY MUSIC

Strictly speaking, 'contemporary' music is that which is composed during the lifetime of the user of the term, but, particularly in this century, much music is written in idioms that were coined some time ago. This is not the place for a discussion as to the validity of works written 'out of their time' and I mention the fact merely to clarify the term as I use it here. In this century music has experienced an historically unparalleled 'explosion,' so that greater changes have taken place within the average person's lifetime than occurred in any previous century – or more. Who, in 1900, would have foreseen the advent of dodecaphony, aleatory or *musique concrete*, all of which are now in varying degrees *passé*? The hard truth is, and maybe has always been, that each of us reaches a point at which we begin to distinguish between 'music' and 'non-music,' two categories separated by a third, that of music with which we can still identify to some extent and which still says something of value to us – though we would not feel comfortable, or even able, to play or compose it. The leading edge of the *avant garde* (tomorrow's *arriere garde!*) has gone beyond the limits of our comprehension. To most people this 'no-man's land' and the 'non-music' constitute 'contemporary' music, though it would be more accurate to define 'contemporary' music as that which *could not* have been written in any earlier time.

The point at which one cuts off depends on very many things, of which age, temperament and open-mindedness are only three. The kinds of music which surround one during one's formative years, objects of special affection, are likely to establish a base-line from which to measure those that follow, not least when the latter represent radical changes that challenge the very bases of our established ethics. Segovia was 'formed' in a climate of Romanticism, which accorded with his own nature, and he 'cut off' at quite an early stage. Debussy, Ravel and even, in his early phase, Schoenberg, retained in their music those elements to which Segovia subscribed, but Bartók, Stravinsky [11] and Berg were among those who did not. In seeking to expand the guitar's repertory Segovia approached many living composers, but they were those who were classifiable as '(late-) romantic' or 'neo-classical' – begin with Torroba, Turina, Manén, Castelnuovo-Tedesco, Ponce and Rodrigo. Alexandre Tansman, some of whose music appeared *'avant-garde'* to Segovia, was told: "When you write for the guitar you must first wipe your pen clean." Frank Martin was less fortunate; his *Quatre pièces brèves*, now standard repertory, were rejected as "not music," after which chastening experience he never again wrote for the guitar. [12] Roussel's *Segovia* won the maestro's approval but Milhaud's *Segoviana* did not! These examples might be multiplied but, together with the following few anecdotes, they will suffice.

1) One evening in 1968, as I drove him from his hotel to my home, I asked if he had heard the Nocturnal of Benjamin Britten. He had: "It is *arid*. Instead of making a beautiful tree (his left arm swept in the direction of Regents Park, past which we were driving) he has made a lamp-post!" – his right arm, gesturing towards an example of such an artifact, crossed my field of vision, passing just in time for me to evade an approaching traffic island, contact with which might have changed the course of our history. In his last years he came to accept "some movements" of the *Nocturnal*, but he never said (to me) which they were. The work is now one of the finest the guitar has yet received but, before censuring Segovia, who was 75 years old at that time, we should note that there are still young guitarists who find the *Nocturnal* incomprehensible and/or unacceptable – and some leading virtuosi who have yet to play it in public. Think carefully before you cast your stone!

2) In the early 1980s I commented to Segovia that he had not played in Paris for a long time. He explained: "André Jolivet has written a piece, a homage to De Visée. I know I am old-fashioned, but it makes my eyes feel funny just to look at it! If I go to Paris he will ask me about it."

3) Sometime in the early 1980s I played him the recording of Nikita Koshkin's *Andante quasi passacaglia* and *Toccata ("The fall of birds")* by Vladimir Mikulka, which provoked the response: "What a piece it is – and what a player! But the *Toccata* is full of the confusion that is in the Russian mind!" I took the latter

statement as his way of expressing less-than-total approval and did not ask him to explain it! Koshkin's use of the guitar is adventurous, but his musical language falls far short of the *avant garde.*

4) I have written music in many styles, some of which Segovia did not like; there were works that I did not even bother to show to him since his reaction was predictable. He equated Art with Beauty and Nobility, and any form of unpleasantness (as he defined it) was foreign to it; only the mildest and most time-honored dissonance was permissible. I am sure that he would have been happy in a world in which Good alone prevailed (wouldn't we all?!), without need of Evil to define it by antithesis. I played him a tape of my *Tout en ronde, Op. 57,* splendidly performed by John Mills – Segovia's most faithful spiritual disciple, after which he said: "It is very good – but I like the second and third movements better; they are more preetier." The first movement contains a few mild dissonances! At the end of the last (phone) conversation I ever had with him, in late 1986, he said: "Continue to write *good* music. Do not join the league of the bad composers."

In finding much of the music written in his own lifetime to be unpleasant, unacceptable and barren, he was not alone. A like conservatism is apparent in the repertoires of many of today's leading performers, who differ from him only in degree and date of 'cut-off,' prisoners in their own, different cages, as indeed we all are.

NINETEENTH-CENTURY MUSIC

In essence there was little difference between Segovia's interpretative approaches to the music of the classic guitar's 'adolescence' and to any other. If he evinced no particular interest, or showed much sign of being concerned with, the use of period instruments, fingerings or techniques (much of which could have been applied without removal of one's right-hand fingernails), then neither did anyone else who was visible above the horizon. His performances of this music must be regarded in much the same way as those of pre-classical music. Even more, he would have seen later instruments and practices, the vehicles that carried the music, as the culmination of a line of evolution that relegated their earlier counterparts to obsolescence. Academic and practical concern with historical verity in this field has now gained much momentum, but many concert performers remain minimally touched by it, content to inherit anachronisms from their elders. Certainly, the facsimile editions now available were not so in the bulk of Segovia's lifetime, nor was the facility of being able to request photocopies of material held in libraries or museums; the location of original manuscripts or first editions required laborious effort, and when they were tracked down they still had to be studied *in situ*. Segovia is unlikely to have been deeply involved in such academic pursuits.

A well-publicized example of discrepancy and apparent meddling is the edition of 20 of Sor's Studies by Segovia, one that is still in use throughout the world. Several of the Studies, none of which carries Sor's original opus number, differ radically from what is shown in the first editions [13]; it is not only the note-content that varies – in the case of Op. 31/19 (Segovia No. X) the radical changes in the given fingering destroy the original technical purpose of the piece, carefully stated by Sor.[14] The responsibility for these changes has been laid at Segovia's doorstep, but the charge may be unjustified in some instances. Napoléon Coste published, in 1845, a *"Méthode complète pour la Guitare par Ferdinand Sor, rédigée et augmentée de nombreux exemples et leçons..."* Those who have seen it, of whom I am not yet one, tell me that this is the origin of these changes – a book that Segovia was more likely to have seen than he was any original edition of Sor's Studies. It seems to me, too, that it would not have been within his character to tamper to such an extent with the texts of 'classics,' composed by a great guitarist, a part of the modern instrument's heritage, written in a musical language with which (unlike that of the modal tongue of the *vihuelistas*) he was thoroughly *au fait*, and requiring no translation of tablature. More probably, these were what he *believed* to be Sor's texts.

He did a service to the classic guitar and to its early composers by making this music widely known, investing it with affection and playing it to the best of his ability, though with minimal support of musicological investigation. The performance of earlier musics in historically inappropriate fashions was never exclusively Segovia's province; it still happens occasionally, in recordings and concerts of all kinds – except for those given by artists who are devoted to 'authenticity,' and in an age when ignorance has ceased to be a viable plea.

Overall, Segovia's style varied but minimally with the period of the music he played; his own, strongly romantic vision of music imposed a large degree of uniformity. His freedom with rhythm was less when he played Bach (though not entirely absent) but it invaded all else. One may perhaps be pardoned for a wry smile on reading what he wrote about Ida Presti after her death: "Her fingers sometimes were disobedient to the right tempo." Any use of pronounced rubato or deviation from the pulse on Presti's part was never the consequence of limited technique – to judge as far back as her first recordings, [15] when she was only fourteen years old (1938); it was in accordance with her musical feelings – as it was also with Segovia!

CHAPTER FOUR

Segovia
the guitarist

Exactly what constituted "Segovia's" technique has never been entirely clarified. So many basic elements were already established before his advent: the position of the hands and body, the use of apoyando, the involvement of the nails of the right hand – he invented none of these. What appears to be true is, that he brought together what he considered to be the most desirable of these elements, refining and synthesizing them to meet his ultimate purpose – that of making the guitar as eloquent an instrument of musical expression as he knew how. He had 'students' but they were for the most part players whose techniques were already developed to the point at which they justified exposure to the maestro's attention via musical performances. Though he often commented both favorably and otherwise on their qualities, his master classes were devoted mainly to matters of interpretation. Neither did he write a method: There is a book entitled "The Segovia Technique," [16] but it deals only with certain physical aspects; there is no study material, and the text was not written by Segovia himself! He was in fact not wholly pleased with this book; he told me that when the photographs of his hands were taken, he had believed it was solely for 'archival' purposes, not to provide the framework of a book of instruction. At the same time, he never voiced any specific criticism of the text – even privately to me, let alone publicly.

Another didactic work that bears his name is "Guidance for the beginner. Segovia – my book of the guitar." [17] It contains many *bons mots* and some charming pictures of children, raptly attentive to the maestro's unheard directives, but it contains nothing that is not in many other primers. The rudiments of music begin on page 14, the guitar itself enters on page 22, after which progress from rock-bottom to the studies that appear on page 48 et seq. is so rapid, that teachers will be hard put to relate it to the realities of their working lives. It is a sweet little book, showing the kindly and poetic faces of Segovia, but it is hard to imagine that he *really* regarded it as a serious, thought-through contribution to systematic guitar instruction. The technical "School of Segovia" thus remains undefined, except insofar as it may be pieced together from his various comments and by observation. He left no such concrete legacy.

THE RIGHT HAND

Segovia inherited the turned right wrist from Tárrega and his contemporaries, as many others have since done from him. It should not be forgotten, that for many decades Segovia served as the role model of technical propriety; what he did and how he appeared to do it, was followed by countless others who learned their 'lessons' by observation, perforce at a distance. There were, too, many who imitated him 'photographically' – but few who reasoned out *why* he did things in the way he did; there were even some who aped his hairstyle, walk, dress (down to the shoe-string bow tie) and platform manner, only to find that success demanded rather more than that!

One major shift away from the 'technique of Segovia' in recent decades has been in the maintenance of the right hand more in direct line with the forearm, as occurs naturally when the arm is allowed to hang down passively by the side. One famous guitarist, whose technique remained brilliant and unhampered in his eighth decade, is of the opinion that a major factor in the indisputable (and sad) decline in Segovia's technique, even in *his* eighth decade, was the cumulative wear and tear caused by the angling of his right wrist, carrying the tendons around corners instead of allowing them to run straight from the forearm into the hand. This may be true, though it remains unprovable. What is of paramount importance is the angle of the fingers to the strings, and today's players frequently achieve this by other means, avoiding the angled wrist.

In Segovia's youth the dominant influence on technique was Tárrega, who did not use his right-hand nails, but earlier players had already used the nails in combination with the flesh. Aguado deals with the matter in some detail in his 'New Guitar Method,' [18] and this probably provided Segovia with his starting point; he does not mention Aguado in his autobiography but he constantly stressed the value and importance of his Studies. Whatever the truth, Segovia put the technique to good use, giving a wide variety of beautiful sounds – and in doing so he acted directly against the prevailing tide of Tárrega's no-nails philosophy. His objectives were to produce an 'orchestrally versatile' range of tone-color, and to gain the volume and projection needed for the large concert halls into which he visualized his career as taking him. [19] Although pockets of 'fingernails-in-the-wallpaper' resistance (an ironic simile!) have continued, the tide has not turned against Segovia's approach; no significant concert performer in the world now uses only the fleshy fingertips. Lutenists have long fought over the same battleground but, though the use of right-hand nails is less sternly disapproved than it once was, flesh-only is still favored; their situation is however different from that of guitarists. In laying the fleshy pad of the finger across both strings of a double course, the lutenist can play both simultaneously, instead of in rapid but audible succession; the guitar presents no such problem. One thing is certain: that to reject the use of both flesh and nail, separately and in combination, is to impoverish the available variety of tone-color, the 'orchestral' factor that undeniably enhanced Segovia's performances and contributed to their success. The prismatically colored treatment is of course not apt to all kinds of musics but to reject it totally, in favor of a 'harpsichord-on-one-stop' approach would be to act against both the nature and appeal of the guitar.

In playing *apoyando* strokes Segovia inclined his right hand in the 'traditional' way, so that the string was struck deliberately downwards; a shift of hand position thus accompanied any change from one stroke to the other – *apoyando/tirando*. There are obviously 'mixed' situations in which both strokes are called for in rapid succession, as in the Study Op. 35/22 of Sor (Segovia No. V), and it is impractical to shift the hand back and forth every time; in such passages Segovia played both strokes from one position – close to that of the *tirando*. Later generations of first-class players have realized that this latter practice has much wider application, and does not need to be confined to situations in which it is enforced; this pays dividends in economy of movement. Segovia told me that he acknowledged this – but, he said, at his time of life it was too late for him to change! In making a stroke, Segovia sometimes allowed the tip-segment of the right-hand finger to bend (in a controlled fashion, not passively) and at other times he kept it firm. The choice was governed by the quality of sound he wished to produce. I mention this 'for the record' since there are some players who advocate the keeping of the tip joint firm at all times, whilst at the other end of the spectrum some authors of tutor-books have stated (though one later recanted!) that the fingertips should be allowed to bend passively, using nonsensical parallels such as "like the bristles of a paint brush" and "as when you press a light-switch."

Some of his most luscious sounds were produced by the 'sliding *apoyando*,' the stroke in which the finger slides along the string for some distance, most usually in the direction of the fingerboard, before activating it. It may be that others used this before Segovia, but I know of no documentary evidence of it; the device may possibly be his sole innovative contribution to the technical armory of the guitar. The effect of the sliding action is to 'iron' the string, reducing the proportion of the higher partials that give the sound its cutting edge, and though it is explicable in scientific terms – and might even be foreseen by *a priori* reasoning, it is more probable that Segovia came across it in a practical way, subconsciously (maybe even consciously) relating the movement of the hand to his mental image of, and feelings about, the sound he wished to make. A caressing movement corresponds to a caressing sound.

THE LEFT HAND

Segovia's hands were large and strong but these attributes played a smaller part in his left-hand technique than some might imagine. Strength is helpful only when it is controlled: even the strongest hand will eventually tire and fail if excessive pressure is applied to the strings. The student who learns to press no harder than is necessary in any given situation will have acquired one of Segovia's assets. Anyone shaking hands with him for the first time might have been surprised – and deceived by the softness of his grip: this was a ploy he taught to others who, like himself, might face the repeated experience of shaking hands with a line of people after a recital. Even the strongest hand would tire if every handshake were met with equivalent counter-pressure, with obvious detriment to its well-being. If, however, one offers a limply passive hand, the other party will quickly recognize this and refrain from applying too much force.

Although he had large hands they did not appear to have a correspondingly long stretch. In his edition of the *Prelude BWV 999* of Bach (Schott GA 106) he indicates a fourth-finger barré at the fifth fret, at a point at which Ida Presti (amongst others with smaller hands) did not use one. Further, in scales and general passagework he adhered closely to the principle of 'one finger per fret' ('chromatic'), avoiding where possible a stretch of two frets between adjacent fingers and preferring to change position in order to do so. Again, Ida Presti (whose technique was awe-inspiring) followed the opposite principle: 'Stay in position; if you need to stretch, do it!' Segovia *could* stretch, but he seems not to have found it sufficiently comfortable to do it as a natural 'way of life.' Human hands vary in countless respects, as do the ways in which different people find it comfortable and natural to use them.

I once asked Segovia what guiding principles he followed in fingering a piece. He did not say a word: instead, he took his guitar and played a piece through, very slowly, stopping from time to time to raise unused fingers in the air. What he demonstrated with perfect clarity was the use of 'anchor' and 'guide' fingers, important factors in maintaining a stable and secure left hand. There was an abundance of logic, foresight and experience in his left-hand fingerings, from which a great deal may be learned.

Sometime in the 1950s I heard a broadcast from a festival in which Segovia played the time-honored *Gavotte* from Bach's BWV 1006a – and made a dreadful mess of it! Two days later I was with him at his hotel; he asked whether I had heard the transmission. When I said that I had, he immediately said: "Did you hear what happened in the Bach?" I could not but admit that I had! He went on to explain, that he had recently revised the fingering – but had not had time fully to absorb the changes he had made, so that he fell between two stools. I expressed some surprise that he should have felt impelled to make significant adjustments to the fingering of a piece he had been playing for several decades, and I paraphrase his response: One's view of the best way in which to finger a piece continually changes. What one does at any particular time reflects one's musical, spiritual and technical development. If one arrives at a fingering that one considers to be final and definitive, one is effectively 'dead,' whether or not one is officially declared to be so. In later years I found him with many other of his 'old favorites' on his music desk, in the process of being reworked in this way. It is likely that by the time most of his published editions reached print, he was already using different fingerings, and as time passed this was certainly the case. The fingerings in his editions, most of which pre-date World War II, do not represent 'holy writ'; they were those at which he had arrived *at that juncture.* Even if this were not so, it remains true that fingerings are intensely personal matters; what suits and works well (technically and musically) for one player does not necessarily do so for another. All this said, irrespective of whether one changes or follows them, it is wise to consider Segovia's fingerings carefully, to see what can be learned from them. Never reject them out of hand.

In his conversations with me Segovia always referred to fingerings as being 'expressive' or 'inexpressive' – never 'bad' nor 'good,' though he may have used these latter terms at some other times. Fingering is not merely a means of making the notes easily available to the left hand; it also affects phrasing, articulation, tone-quality and, ergo, expressiveness. I showed him a manuscript copy of my *English Suite,* in which one chord was fingered according to the suggestion of a well-known London guitar teacher – on the basis that it fell smoothly under the fingers. Segovia summarily dismissed it as 'inexpressive,' at the same time proposing another – that in the printed edition, [20] which made it possible, with no more trouble, to apply the vibrato that the musical moment invited; the tighter 'under-the-fingers' solution made this virtually impossible.

GENERAL

Few things are more stupid and profitless than to try to ape the exact physical details of the way in which *any* artist plays; they often derive from personal characteristics that are not common to all mankind. Segovia held his guitar somewhat on its back, with the sound hole pointing upwards rather than forwards, a position that few teachers would advocate. It was enforced by his physical shape and he did not recommend it to others; his comment was that: "A guitarist should not eat *too* well!" Many who have difficulty in establishing a career might consider the advice superfluous!

Another observable trait was the directing of his eyes toward the fingerboard, often following the movements of his left hand. This too is not a thing that is now considered sound practice; guitarists should, like other musicians, be able to play without watching their hands – as one needs to do when reading from a score. Of course, everyone who looks in the direction of their left hand is not necessarily *looking* at it but, increasingly in his later years, Segovia did just that. The nature of his career was such that he rarely, if ever, *needed* to sight-read fluently – as many working guitarists now do when playing with other musicians; on the few occasions when Segovia did play 'in company' he would have had ample time to acquaint himself with his part, and even to memorize it. Working as a soloist he could prepare pieces at his own pace, and did not need to perform anything in public until it was polished to his satisfaction. Returning to his earlier statement, that "It is not possible to sight-read on the guitar": it is perfectly possible to do so, as many players now prove on every day of the average year. What he probably meant was, that one could not read both the fingering and the notes at the same time, though there are now numerous guitarists who can do so. Times have changed. If he meant that one cannot arrive at an optimal fingering with such immediacy, then one cannot reasonably disagree, but this does not prevent one from sight-reading any but the most difficult pieces well enough to gain a fair impression of them. Today's guitarists are growing up in a world with different professional requirements from those which Segovia knew at first hand.

In the last decades of his life Segovia suffered problems with his sight: even in the 1960s he held things very close in order to read them; this could not have made it easy for him to read a score on a music desk. On one occasion he passed me a manuscript copy from which he was working, asking me to verify the pitch of a particular note; it was not written in the best handwriting of all time but it seemed quite clear to me. Not long after that he played in the Royal Festival Hall in London: He walked on-stage as usual, sat down, began to tune his guitar, and then walked off again – and did not reappear for some considerable time. There was naturally some speculation as to the reason, some of it apprehensive, some mischievous. After the recital he explained it to me: He had gone on-stage wearing his general-purpose bifocal glasses, only to find that when he looked at the neck of the guitar it appeared to have a step in it, where the fields of the two lenses met! He could not play under these conditions, so he sent someone to his hotel to fetch his playing glasses. Now if he had been accustomed to playing without looking at the fingerboard he would not have been inconvenienced, but as he grew older he became more conscious of the possibility of making a mistake. While his left hand remained close to one position he did not pay too much attention to it, but when he made a wide change of position his eyes followed his left hand, seeing it safely to its destination.

THE SEGOVIA SOUND

Of all the attributes that made Segovia's playing world-famous, his tone – and the variety of it – was the most readily identifiable. It is not surprising, that many others have tried to imitate it (though he often said: "You should try to be the first 'yourself,' not the 'second Segovia') and to learn its secrets. Neither is it surprising, given the facts, that so much arrant nonsense should have been written about it. Few things about guitar playing are more intimately personal than tone, since it relates so closely to both the physical *and* mental characteristics of the player. On the physical level, it depends primarily on the precise dimensions, proportions and textures of the flesh and nails of the right-hand fingers, and on the ways in which those fingers move naturally; other factors, such as the way in which the string is struck, and the superimposition of vibrato also play determinative roles in tone-production. The character of the fingers and nails impose first-order limitations on what is or is not possible. It has been stated, that the gripping strength of Segovia's left hand contributed to the quality of his tone – another piece of nonsense! Following the guidance of Thomas Mace in his "Musick's Monument" (given to lutenists) a good player always *minimizes* the strength of left-hand pressure, especially when applying vibrato, and many players with smaller and less powerful hands produce strong and rich sounds. Segovia's sound was determined, at grass-root level, by his own, unique physical make-up, one that differed from anyone else's – including *yours*, dear reader!

Tone is also shaped in the mind and spirit. Providing that a player has sufficient control over the physical aspects, he/she will produce the type(s) of tone which best suit his/her personality and aesthetic approach to music – or may even betray their lack of awareness that tone-quality is an integral part of their music-making. Tone-quality can be no less a 'trademark' of a player than any other feature of performance. *Vive les differences!* The ground rules as Segovia showed them to be are, that tone should always be of good quality, and that it should be as widely varied as possible, to give the guitar the rich variety of attractive voices that has helped to endear the instrument to many millions of listeners. It would be better if those who, whether by choice or in consequence of some technical dogma, willingly restrict the range of the guitar's sound possibilities, were to find something different to do with their lives!

Segovia practised for two periods of two-and-a-half hours each day, a discipline that was disrupted only by illness, travel, or some other form of *force majeure*. Each session was divided, approximately midway, by some other activity such as reading or writing correspondence, taking coffee, to release cumulative tension. Because he loved what he was doing, he did not regard practice as a necessary evil or a routine chore, but he *did* recognize that it was essential to the maintenance of the standard of his performances.

Segovia examining a page from the author's transcription of Robert Dowland's A Varietie of Lute-Lessons. *(Photo: Maurice Summerfield, courtesy* Classical Guitar Magazine*)*

CHAPTER FIVE

Segovia
as colleague

The first time I received a call from Segovia for a piece was late in 1949. *The Guitar Review* (New York) was planning to produce a photographic issue, a record of the worldwide guitar scene up to and including the then present. Terry Usher and I were asked for an article on guitar duos, with an accompanying piece for two guitars; what we sent was an arrangement of Mozart's *Eine kleine Nachtmusik.* On seeing what we had sent, Segovia approved the article but said that the music was unsuitable, though well arranged: he thought that the issue [21] would reach the eyes of non-guitarist musicians and, as this was the only piece of music it would contain, he did not want them to think that the guitar had nothing but arrangements to offer. "Therefore, ask Mr. Duarte to send one of his original compositions." The news came by letter, with the request that the piece should be sent "by return of post." The problem was that I had never written anything for two guitars, so I immediately retired to the lounge and wrote a piece using only the piano (on which my abilities are extremely rudimentary), and thus was born the *Chanson Op. 14* (published as one of 'Six friendships for two guitars.' [22] This was well received and Bobri reported that, when it arrived. Segovia worked until the small hours of the morning to finger it; as this was only hearsay, and the fingering was not attributed to Segovia when it appeared, I did not mention it when the piece was published, nor did I ever remember to ask him about it.

The project of 1950, relating to my *Prelude Op. 13/1* (page 7), was my first direct experience of any kind of working relationship with Segovia; that it proved fruitless was unimportant, for it was a sign of the way in which his mind worked – though one which I did not 'read' at the time. Most working guitarists are eager to receive new works from composers they like, and do not hesitate to ask for them even when, unlike Segovia, they have little or nothing to offer in return. His mind was constantly active and his requests were always focused, in that he never asked simply for 'a work' or 'a piece' but, rather, for something more or less specific.

Some of his ideas (most usually those made with the tongue somewhere in the cheek) flowed spontaneously from the conversational topic of the moment, as for instance:

1) I had 'introduced' him to the jazz guitarist Wes Montgomery (I was probably the only person who ever played Montgomery's records to him!) and I explained that, not only was he musically unschooled and unable to read notation, but he played everything with downstrokes of his right-hand thumb. Having expressed astonishment and, maybe surprisingly to some, admiration, he said: "You should write a study to be played only with the thumb." As there are already many studies that might be played in that way if so designated, I took a raincheck.

2) We had been discussing the tonal variety of the guitar and I had referred to some passages in his recording of Rodrigo's *Fantasía para un gentilhombre*. This prompted him to comment that, although the guitar could mimic – or at least evoke other instruments such as the cello, bassoon and trumpet, in the presence of the instruments themselves the guitar's range shrank and the illusion was lost. So, he said: "Write a concerto for the guitar *without* orchestra." Bach had, of course, long ago established precedents with his solo-harpsichord *Concerto in the Italian style BWV 971* and his several *Concerti 'after Vivaldi,'* but I did not follow them.

Most often he would however arrive in London with his ideas at the ready, sometimes telephoning me to offer them, sometimes waiting until we met. The following are just a few of those I best remember:

1) A late-evening telephone call announced that: "Rodrigo has written for me a piece in the shadow of *Torre bermeja*; would you also write one? The idea appealed to me and not long afterwards I completed my *Fantasia and fugue on 'Torre bermeja' Op. 30* (1960). [23] At the same time I was puzzled by his request; he had,

to my knowledge, never played Rodrigo's work – and would probably never play mine either! So I did not write with any such expectation, nor did I hesitate to incorporate passages that might not have been to Segovia's taste. I knew too that the resulting piece would have been too taxing for his eyesight and memory at that juncture. He was, however, pleased to receive it, and it has since been performed several times by others. I later made cautious enquiries about this to Rodrigo. He wrote a piece for the piano, *"A l'ombre de Torre bermeja"* in 1946, a posthumous homage to the pianist Ricardo Viñes, a quarter of a century before Segovia's call to me, and he never even considered making an arrangement of it for the guitar. He remains as mystified as I am, as to why Segovia should have spoken as though such a version existed. The mystery deepens and, as the only one who knew the answer is now dead, it must remain unexplained!

2) Early in 1965 he suggested that I should write a book of studies, which I did with little delay. [24] It turned out to be of a technical rather than musical nature. At one point I said to him that I would have liked to include some exercises in arpeggio patterns through chord inversions but that, since he was then giving such exercises to his summer-school students, the idea was his and not mine. He said: "No, you must include them. There is no patent on the dominant seventh." I agreed but said I would acknowledge their origin in the book, but he said this was unnecessary. When he had had the finished manuscript for some time he asked me to see him at his hotel one evening; I arrived at the appointed time, between nine and ten o'clock, only to be told by the hall porter that Segovia was in the restaurant and that I should wait. After more than an hour passed without sight of him (he could not have gone from the restaurant to his room unobserved from where I was waiting), so I

asked again and it was then established that he was in fact in his room and had been there all the time. Having by then concluded that I was not coming, he met me at his room door in his pajamas and dressing gown, and with his usual friendliness and courtesy. After some conversation he wrote the endorsement the published book bears.

3) During one meeting at his hotel he asked me to write something for Emilita, saying that she was "lazy to practise" because "she did not want people to think that she married me in order to get free guitar lessons!" To emphasize the point he asked her to play for me, which she did (the *Prelude* of the Third Cello Suite of Bach) very well indeed. However, I sensed that Emilita would in all events have her own way, and I never got round to doing it. Was I right? Who knows!

4) When Segovia came to London late in 1967 he said: "I think it would be a good idea if you and Castelnuovo-Tedesco were each to write an original theme so that the other might write variations on it. Do you agree?" Whilst I did, I had no idea what Castelnuovo-Tedesco's reaction might be, so I let the matter rest there until, in late February 1968, I received a theme from Castelnuovo-Tedesco, to whom Segovia had obviously spoken in the meantime. There was no time-frame and, as far as I knew, no urgency, so I did not hurry to post anything to Beverly Hills. In fact there was more urgency than I could have realized: his theme for me was dated 18 February, and on 17 March he died. He was a very methodical man and it was his habit, before going to bed, to lay out on his desk the music he would work on the next day, the letters he would answer – often accompanied by the envelopes ready addressed for his replies. One night he addressed an air-letter form to me but by the next day he was dead. His widow, Clara,

found it and sent it to me later – a last, unspoken greeting from the grave, kept unanswered in my archives. I did not immediately 'see my way into' a guitar solo work on this theme and as, again, there seemed to be no reason to hurry, I laid it aside. Segovia made no further reference to the project and the theme remained unused until 1978 when, in response to a request from Raymond Burley and Stephen Bell for a new work for guitar and harpsichord, I returned to it. To mark the work's association with two composers (one an Italian), two players and two different instruments, I gave it the title *Insieme* ("together") under which it is published. [25]

5) Though he had great affection for flamenco, in its earlier and less flamboyant form, he was always very conscious of what he saw as the need to keep a distance between the classic guitar and its flamenco brother. In particular he eschewed 'noise' in the form of heavy strumming or the *rasgueado*, which he regarded as features of folk performance, not 'proper' to the guitar's art-musical status. He was enthusiastic about my *Variations on a Catalan folksong Op. 25* but not about the chord-tremoloed, 'grandstand' finish to the finale. He asked me to rewrite the offending passages in a different form, so that he could play the work; I did so, he pronounced his entire satisfaction with the result – but he never did play it! The general success of the piece may have been the reason for this: He had told me, in another connection, that he had never played one particular and extremely famous concerto because he did not like some passages (which, coincidentally, contained similar writing) and, though they could have been rewritten to his taste, the work was too well known in its existing form to make a substantially changed version viable.

6) One day in 1973 he telephoned to tell me that he had been asked several times to perform Paganini's six *Centone di Sonate* with various distinguished violinists, but had refused because the partnership was so unequal; the violin had all the interesting music, the guitar part was of student level. Now he had been asked again, this time to play them with Ruggero Ricci, for whom he had special regard – and whose wife played the guitar and was nicknamed 'Shegovia.' Therefore, would I please rewrite the guitar parts in such a way that the two instruments were brought to a comparable level. It was clear to me that there was no realistic chance that the performance would ever take place: to read his part from the score would have been beyond the capacity of Segovia's eyesight, the task of memorizing so much music for the purposes of one 'star' concert would have been disproportionately taxing, and Segovia was unused to playing in an equal partnership with any other virtuoso – a situation in which, moreover, his proneness to memory lapses would have proved disastrous. Obvious as it was, it was unthinkable to point this out to Segovia and, as I found the proposed exercise interesting, I arranged the first of the six and sent it to him as a 'sampler'; he appears not to have received it. Early in 1974 it was 'field-tested' in Cecilia Peijel's debut concert in Uppsala (Sweden) and found to be effective, so I addressed myself to the second and fourth Sonate (the third was not a suitable case for treatment) and, feeling that enough was enough, did no more. Some time after that he told me that the date and venue of the heralded concert were fixed, and that I would be invited to New York to be present. At this point I still retained sufficient doubt to delay work on the remaining three pieces, and it proved justified. A later call told me that, having heard some Paganini violin/guitar works played in London by Ithzak Perlman and John Williams, he had concluded that such

a combination did not work successfully in a concert hall – the violin was too powerful for the guitar. The end-point had always been predictable, though the manner of its attainment had not been; the work was however not wasted, the three completed *Sonate* were published [26] appropriately, in Italy, and two have been superbly recorded in Japan by Yoko Fujita and Shin-Ichi Fukuda.

7) In another amusing situation arising out of 'imbalance' it was Segovia who found himself in the 'heavier pan': he asked Alexandre Tansman to write a piece for guitar and harp, so that he might play it in concert with Nicanor Zabaleta (whose role in relation to the harp was akin to that of Segovia's with the guitar in this century). Tansman told me that, entertaining the same doubts I had had with regard to the Paganini enterprise, he did not propose to devote much effort to producing a work for a concert that would probably never take place. He had accordingly solved his problem by merely adding a subsidiary, accompanying harp part to his *Suite in modo polonico*, which would permit Segovia to play what he already knew. Unsurprisingly, the prospect of playing Legnani to Segovia's Paganini did not appeal to Zabaleta, one more reason why the mooted concert never happened. The harpist Marisa Robles asked me if I knew of any original work for guitar and harp (the occasion was the press launch of Segovia's autobiography in 1977); I told her of Tansman's piece and suggested she ask Segovia where the score might be found. If she ever came by it, her reaction may have been the same as Zabaleta's; I never heard any more of it.

8) Segovia asked me many times to arrange some English folksongs or to write something based on them; he was as fond of them as the English more usually are of those of almost *any* other

country! I did arrange and publish some arrangements, though I am not sure that I ever showed them to him – nor can I remember *why* I did not. Sometime in the late 1950s I had written a small piece, mostly composed in my head to pass the time while driving home from Central London one evening, one I then visualized as the first of a set of 'Fairy-tales' – an attractive title used by the Russian composer Nikolay Medtner for many of his piano pieces. I do not remember giving a copy of it to Segovia (maybe someone else did!) but he certainly had one, for he produced it, pronounced it as "fresh and spontaneous," and said that if I would add two more movements, one slow and song-like and the other dance-like, he would play the whole work. Thus was born the English Suite that has dogged my footsteps ever since, as *Estrellita* did Ponce's and the Prelude in C♯ minor did Rachmaninov's.

When it was completed he said: "You will be astonished at the success it will have." I was, to say the least, sceptical, but his judgment proved better than mine!

THE ENGLISH SUITE

The little piece, by then notionally renamed 'Prelude' (like 'Study,' a convenient title for a detached oddment), was very short – it corresponded to the E-major flanking sections of the final Prelude, and I realized that this would determine the dimensions of the finished work: one could scarcely have a brief Prelude followed by two lengthy movements. When I began thinking about the work it occurred to me that I could use it to kill two birds with one stone: by using English folksong material in the other two movements I could justify the title of 'English Suite,' thus satisfying another of Segovia's wishes. The second movement was a simple presentation of a folksong "Bushes and briars"; the main material of the third movement was of my own invention but with an English folksong ("The ballad of Robin Hood") embedded in the central section. Both were, to maintain proportion with the Prelude, brief, especially the slow movement. I gave the manuscript to Segovia and silence reigned until his next visit to London, maybe half a year later, when his verdict was that: "Torroba and I think that the second movement is too short. Can you please write something longer." What I had foreseen had begun to come to pass! I thus wrote an entirely new second movement, in which the outer sections were based on an English folksong ("The cuckoo") and the central one was entirely original. The first-offered slow movement is now one of "Three English folksongs" [27] in which it appears exactly as I first wrote it. Time again passed until, again in London, Segovia reported: "The slow movement is very beautiful. Torroba and I feel that the *first* movement is now too short. Can you insert another section in the middle, in another key, to lengthen it?" Full marks to my crystal ball! I did so, completing the 'folkloricisation' of the work by introducing yet another folksong ("Low down in the broom"). The next stage was a session of about three hours in his hotel room, during which he played the Suite to me and indicated a number of left-hand fingerings that differed from the ones I had marked, all of which emphasized the subtlety of his mind in this area; this was done in order that I might include them in the published edition that was shortly to go into preparation. I give one example: I originally conceived the passage in the second movement which begins with bar 2 of system 2 on page 4 of the published score [28] as being played across the fingerboard in the second position, as numerous students have presented it to me in classes – probably under the impression that they have made a discovery. This fingering lies more comfortably under the fingers than the published one, Segovia's, but it is less expressive and it yields a less homogeneously warm quality of sound – *c.f.* the change mentioned on page —. He also suggested two minor changes in the score itself, to which I agreed; ironically, he had returned to my original in one of these by the time he first performed the work in the Fairfield Halls, Croydon! It is easy to remember the date of this meeting (22 November 1963): as I left the Westbury Hotel, the lift-attendant gave me the stop-press news that President Kennedy had been assassinated!

Agreement having been reached on all details, and with the dedication of the work "to Andrés Segovia and his wife on the occasion of their marriage," the maestro's cup of contentment was full – well, almost! Shortly before the premiere he suggested that the second movement would be even better if I were to insert a (preferably modulatory) passage between the first and second statements of the second (my own) theme; I did so but it was, of course, too late to be included in the first performances – it does, however, appear in both the printed score (Novello) and Segovia's recording of the work. The third movement was the only one to survive exactly as I first wrote it. Segovia's interpretation on the record is not the one I had in my mind when I wrote the Suite but it is a beautiful one, the one (of 12) to which I first turn when playing the work to someone else. As I am a phlegmatic Englishman, and Segovia was a romantically inclined Spaniard who was 26 years my senior, it would have been remarkable had we 'heard' the piece in exactly the same way; it would also have been a negation of the valid variety that is what music is all about! But then I have never once heard any piece of mine played (on record or in concert) in precisely the way I visualized it. That is perhaps the way it *should* be.

Chapter Five

The experience was instructive and enjoyable in every way. Those of other composers who wrote for Segovia but did not understand the guitar in detail must have been even more instructive; at least I never confronted him with anything that was impractical, let alone impossible. If these latter should or could have been instructive they may not always have proved to be so: Segovia told me of two very famous non-guitarist composers whose works he played but, he said, had "never learned to write properly for the guitar." I will not name them!

He also told me, in relation to both the *English Suite* and my arrangement of the Bach Suite, that he did not want to make any change of which the author did not specifically approve. In his collaborations with me he kept faith with this principle, even to the extent of suppressing changes to both works with which I did not agree. Nevertheless works do have a way of 'evolving' over the years in the hands of guitarists, especially their dedicatees, and Segovia continued to the end to make changes to many works, even to their titles, some by composers who had long departed to meet their Maker. It would not surprise me to learn that he had their telephone numbers in Eternity! Changes of this kind to the text are always liable to occur when a work by a non-guitarist composer is tested over a period of time in the laboratory of concert performance, and Segovia has not been alone in making them. Sometime in 1979 I talked to him about, *inter alia*, the *Petite Valse* of Ponce and, having seen it represented on a record sleeve as "arranged by Segovia," asked whether it was in fact originally written for the guitar. He said that it certainly was, one of three pieces Ponce wrote in response to his request for something light and tuneful for use as an encore (*Mazurca* and *Tropico* were the other two), adding that, when a composer who does not really understand the guitar writes for it, the score must *always* be adapted. An extreme case appears to have been the last movement of the *Sonatina meridional*: the one which Ponce first wrote was declared (by Segovia) to be unplayable on the guitar. Ponce accepted this judgment and said that he would bring another one "the day after tomorrow," which he did; this was the one that appears in the published edition. Segovia never told me what had happened to the discarded movement, nor did it occur to me to ask him!

No matter how wise such modifications may be it is still interesting, and archivally valuable, to know just what the composer did originally write, but this is seldom possible if the manuscript remains in the possession of the player for whom the work was written or is otherwise hidden from view. In the case of many works that are now standard repertory we shall probably never know how much Segovia changed what the composers wrote, though if the music is good we may feel that the heart does not need to grieve too much over what the eye can never see. His propensity for making *ad hoc* changes to his concert programmes did not make life easy for the writer(s) of his concert-programme notes: on one occasion, for example, I telephoned to him in Madrid concerning a mysterious item from Castelnuovo-Tedesco's *Platero y yo*, which he was scheduled to play; he had identified it only by the tempo marking. As there were two movements that were so marked, I asked him which it would be; he obliged, confirming it by humming the tune. I framed the programme note around this, but on the night it was the other one that he played!

For many years I had speculated about the 12 *Preludes* of Manuel Ponce (Schott GA 124-5): they traverse some keys that are seldom found in guitar music, and only one is repeated – the first and last pieces are in F♯ minor. Could it have been that Ponce planned to follow Bach (and others) in writing one in each of the major and minor keys, in which case there should have been 24, and that the project failed for some reason to be completed? Did Ponce stop in mid-stream, rounding off the set by returning tidily to the first key? In 1972 I asked these questions, to which Segovia simply replied: "Yes, it was something like that" and offered no further elucidation. Since then the original manuscripts of these 12 *Preludes*, and of 11 others, have been located; they are published, together with a notional twenty-fourth, and edited by Miguel Alcázar. [29] What emerges is that Segovia clearly selected those he liked and published them; in the process he also made some alterations to the texts and changed the keys of many of them. In my view he improved them by so doing, but why he seems to have rejected some of the others is not easy to understand. Miguel Alcázar is at present carrying out a comparative study of Ponce's original manuscripts versus Segovia's printed editions; his lecture on the subject at the 1987 Festival of the Guitar Foundation of America (in Tempe, Arizona) indicates that his findings, should they be published, will make absorbing reading!

It is as reflexive to wax indignant about such 'meddlings' as it was for Pavlov's dogs to answer their dinner-bells, but the matter is not *quite* so simple. When a work is written by a composer whose knowledge of the guitar is at best limited, it is more than likely that there will be passages that are unplayable or which, without sacrificing the composer's aesthetic intentions, may be made more effective by introducing some changes. There are only three possible ways of dealing with the situation: (1) to publish exactly what the composer wrote, the *Urtext*, as Angelo

Gilardino has done with some of the works of Castelnuovo-Tedesco. In this case every performer will arrive at his/her own solution, producing many versions of the music – exactly *what* then would constitute the work? (2) for the work to be published in different editions, prepared by different virtuosi and representing a cross-section of opinion. This would raise the same question as (1) and would in any case be in breach of Copyright Law. (3) for the work to be published in the edition of one reputable performer, preferably the one who has collaborated with the composer and has his blessing. This is precisely what happens in most cases, whether the editor be Segovia or Federico Pluckoso, and no better solution to the problem has yet been devised. The same criteria largely apply to arrangements of music written for other instrumental media, not least that of Granados, Albéniz, Falla *et al*, the untouched scores of which are freely available for consultation and of which widely differing guitar arrangements are on the market. Let the player who never changed *anything* in the printed score be the first to point an accusing finger in Segovia's or anyone else's direction. When changes are made after the composer's death but are said to have met with his earlier approval we are on ground that must, in an imperfect world, remain unsure. The relatively simple theme of Castelnuovo-Tedesco on which I based *Insieme* was impracticable as he wrote it. By the time I composed the work he was unavailable for consultation. Should I have created a precedent by publishing also the Urtext version of the theme? With all due respects, I think not.

In time Copyright Protection lapses and any composer's work becomes Public Domain. Providing the composers' manuscripts are located it will be fascinating to see the new editions of music by, say, Ponce (1998), Tansman (2036), Castelnuovo-

Tedesco (2018), Turina (1999) and Torroba (2034) prepared by 'new Segovias'; if the originals remain undiscovered then the identity of the new editors' '*Urtexten*' will be as obvious as that they will, from a purist's point of view, be 'polluted.'

My own relationship with Segovia in this area was different from that of most other composers in that I understand very well how the guitar works; I have however no reason to believe that, in musical matters, my experience was radically different from that of those whose understanding was minimal. He was deeply sensitive to musical nuance, profoundly experienced in the practicalities of the guitar – and their relationship to the music, and he cared attentively about every minute detail. Where he felt that something might, as he saw it, be better, he had a positive alternative to propose and he was at pains to explain his reasons – but at the same time ready to give way if it was not approved. Those earlier composers must have been delighted by the skills he brought to their collaborations, inspired by his incandescent passion, stimulated by the prospect of writing for an 'old' instrument that had, as they must have seen it, become 'new' in Segovia's hands, and in many cases grateful that the propagation of their music by him was opening new doors for them. It does not seem likely that any of them would have objected much, if at all, to any changes he proposed; rather would they have deferred to his knowledge of the guitar and of what best suited or was even practicable on it. One significant difference between our own time and that in which Segovia was encouraging non-guitarist composers to write for him is that, whereas many of those who wrote for him became far more famous through their guitar music than they might have done through their other works, the reputations of many of those who have written at the prompting of other, later-generation guitarists (Britten, Tippett, Ginastera, Arnold, Walton, Henze and others) have in no measurable way depended on their guitar works. If you doubt this, look them all up in the catalogues of gramophone recordings, a good test of a composer's fame; in how many cases do recordings of their non-guitar works outnumber those of their guitar music? It is likely however that these distinguished, later composers might never have written at all for the guitar had Segovia not shown the instrument to be worthy of their attention – and fostered the development of other guitarists who could justify it by their own performances.

I believe I am the only English composer with whom Segovia ever collaborated in this way, and there can be few others of *any* nationality who did so – and are still alive to tell their tales. The letters exchanged between Segovia and Manuel Ponce reveal something of their collaborative relationship, but not the details and the precise motivations – how did they (Ponce in particular) *really* feel about the changes that were made? To what extent did he suppress his innermost feelings in dealing with an artist who was not only his close friend, but also one who was playing such an important part in the spreading of his (Ponce's) fame in the world – the 'gratitude factor'? We can never know. Such 'horse-trading' between composer and performer happens every day, but only when the latter is a charismatic and forceful key-figure such as Segovia is much public curiosity aroused!

❧

CHAPTER SIX

Segovia
the man

Musical performance reflects instrumental competence but it also tells us a great deal about the performer him- or herself; the way one plays and the way one is are inextricably interconnected. The statement by a famous guitarist, that: "Bad people cannot make good music" is somewhat simplistic – how, for instance, do we define 'bad'? – but there is nevertheless a measure of truth in it. One's approach to and performance of music are revelatory of oneself, providing the listener knows how to assess what he/she hears. An evaluation of any great artist would be incomplete without some consideration of his/her character and temperament – and Segovia is no exception.

Some years ago one of my students 'introduced' a psychologist of his acquaintance to Segovia, of whom the latter knew nothing (yes, there were and are such people!), by means of a recording on which the maestro both played and spoke, and showing him a photograph. The psychologist summed up his experience thus: "In all my professional career I have never encountered such a king-size ego!" It matters little whether this was a measure of Segovia's ego or of the limitedness of the psychologist's experience, what is important is to understand what part an artist's 'ego' plays in his/her functioning – and to realize that the term is not in itself pejorative. Anyone who does *anything* before an audience – whether it be any form of entertainment, after-dinner speaking, lecturing or acting simply as a master of ceremonies – *must* have an ego, no matter how small, for they are saying, in effect: "I have something worthwhile to say. Listen!" It does not, of course, follow that everyone who has an ego also has something worthy of an audience's attention – that would be a false syllogism, nor is it true that everyone who has something of value to offer also has the self-confidence to confront others with it – I have heard many fine 'dressing room' players whose abilities suffered thrombosis in the presence of an audience; it is, too, easier for the composer because he/she is not *obliged* to come face to face with the public. No performer who is worth the hearing can, however, function without ego.

Ego must also be distinguished from egotism. An artist may have a strong ego yet remain free from conceit, be genuinely interested in and caring for others, and even be haunted by a measure of insecurity. In response to something Segovia had said during dinner on 4 November 1949 Olga Coelho commented: "Andrés, you are conceited!" He countered with: "No, my dear, I am not conceited – but I do know my own worth!" Conceit is the *overvaluation* of one's worth and I do not believe Segovia was guilty of this. It is perhaps less certain than he may have believed, that his oft-expressed, youthful ambitions on the guitar's behalf were entirely fulfilled, but he could not have pursued them in any practical way had he had not possessed the necessary faith in himself (= ego). There were, as some are wont to point out, other great guitarists who were active during the years in which Segovia carved his (and the guitar's) niche – the 1920s-1950s, including Emilio Pujol, Miguel Llobet, Agustin Barrios and Ida Presti (whose instrumental and musical talents were not less than Segovia's), but public awareness of them on any but a 'regional' front ranged from minimal to nil. What they might, could, or even *should* have done is idle speculation; for a variety of reasons their achievements in no way matched Segovia's in terms of propagating the guitar on a global scale. It has been said that Segovia promoted himself as much as he did the guitar, but to what extent this is true seems to me unimportant; that he did so much for the instrument is enough, and he surely deserved recognition for it. During those early decades he was the only guitarist whose name was known to the general musical public – and, for that matter, to very many guitar aficionados; that mould was broken by the emergence of Julian Bream.

To the end he remained, however, the supreme Father Figure of the guitar. One evening in the late 1960s, as I was driving him from my home to his hotel, he made some mildly disparaging remark about amateurs. I pointed out to him that the guitar was not maintained by him, either alone or together with the other virtuosi of the day, but by the uncounted amateurs who formed the base of the pyramid – those who bought records, concert tickets, guitars, strings and copies of the *Chaconne* of Bach which they would never be able to play properly. After a moment's consideration he said: "Yes, Jack, you are right. But if there were not so many sinners there would be no need for a Pope!" – to which I could think of no effective response. He was a master of the art of conceding the game but winning the match.

If he was technically and musically 'the right man, born at the right time' to revive the guitar's fortunes, he was no less so in his personal attributes. His physical dimensions – height and, in his later years, breadth, and his dignified mien made him an imposing figure, yet it was apparent that behind the sternly serious expression there lurked a softer and more benign core, shown in the gentle humor of his closing 'addresses' – "I would like to continue, but the guitar is tired" and the like, which his audiences learned to expect. The ability to strike an adept balance between dignity and friendliness was undoubtably helpful in the formation of his career; he could and did mix with people of all conditions – from kings to the most vapid 'fans,' putting them *all* at ease and making even the least of them feel that they mattered. At the same time it was not possible to lose sight of the fact that he was a man of unusual importance, not to be treated casually; the net result was the maintenance of what Julian Bream has referred to as a 'distance' between himself and his public – albeit a friendly one. A great artist needs to be seen as a genuine and recognizable human being – but at the same time a 'special' one; this might be one definition of good public relations. Segovia's platform manner was dignified and unpretentiously authoritative and 'paternal'; in his playing he remained statue-like and made few demonstrative gestures. His premise was that the artist's function was to act as the music's mouthpiece, not to draw attention away from it by his/her actions. In the early 1950s I asked about various members of the Society of the Classic Guitar in New York, where I had not yet been. He said that he had recently attended a meeting of the Society, at which he arrived late – when one of them was in the course of playing a piece. As he entered, the man looked up and acknowledged Segovia with a friendly salute: "He should not have done it. He should have been concentrating on the music and should not have noticed me. It was *vulgar*." On many occasions, people who were well known to him sat dead-center in the front row, where he could not have failed to see them, yet his face never flickered in their direction. Had the reincarnation of J.S. Bach appeared, seated under his nose one evening, I doubt that he would have shown any reaction – though he might have been inspired to play even better!

He was, in fact, opposed to any kind of gesture, even involuntary, that might draw attention to the performer. I was aware of this when, one evening in 1976, I asked one of my best students to play for him. Staffan Kåge (Swedish) played very musically indeed and with excellent technique, but he was prone to accompany his performances with facial contortions such as those for which Julian Bream has been well known. As Staffan (like Julian) was not aware of them when playing, I considered (I still do) them as irrelevant to the main issue – that of a technically secure and sensitive performance, so I arranged a standard lamp in such a position that, with Staffan sitting immediately in front of it, Segovia would not see his face clearly. The ploy was successful – but I had forgotten something: Staffan, again like Julian, was given to tapping his right foot on the floor. Segovia, noticing this, levered himself down into his armchair and tried to put his left foot on Staffan's 'pedal metronome.' He could not quite reach so he resumed his original position, reached for his famous silver-topped walking stick and placed its lower end on the offending foot. If Staffan noticed it he did not register the fact or stop playing. At the end of the performance Segovia complimented him warmly on what he had heard, but added: "You know, some people have the beat in their heads. Some have the beat in their feet. A *musician* has it in his *heart*!" It was not the time to mention that Julian Bream, whose musicianship Segovia greatly admired, was a paid-up member of the Foot-tappers' Union, or to ask whether a musician might not have the beat in all three places at the same time!

Somewhat provocatively, I once told Segovia that he, and every other performer of music of any kind, was in 'show business.' His eyebrows rose by several centimeters but he waited for me to continue. I explained that the important difference between a concert performance and a recorded one is the presence of the artist, the visual element that gives it immediacy, and that the personality and comportment of the performer are thus obviously important. Different artists 'show' themselves in different, individual ways, and can go a long way toward influencing the audience's response before they have even sat down or played a note. He said: "Yes, that is right. I had never thought of it that way before." Whether by instinct or by design, Segovia was, in the best possible sense, a master of show business.

SILENT COMMUNICATION

Segovia could communicate a great deal without needing to say it: one always knew the moment when, at the end of an evening, he was ready to go back to his hotel – even before he spoke, and it was the same when he was ready to terminate a meeting on his own ground. There was often no perceptible gesture, but one still knew that the time had come! This ability to regulate comings and goings so smoothly, without making others feel uncomfortable, must have been very useful to him: During the 1950s in particular he often received a succession of visitors for business or social purposes, arriving at specified times. In these he 'held court' in the lounge of the Piccadilly Hotel, each visitor arriving at his/her allotted time and partaking of light refreshment, supplied at the kinds of price that only such places know how to charge without blushing – given my salary at that time I would not have cared to pay Segovia's total bill for such casual entertaining. The well-lubricated change-overs were an education in the art of public relations; those departing knew, without looking at their watches, when the moment had come – but that it did not mean that they had outstayed their welcome. In 1970, the year in which his youngest son, Carlos Andrés, was born, Segovia was interviewed in London by almost everyone with access to a tape-recorder or with shorthand skill. Of the numerous published interviews, the two-page centre-spread in the *Daily Mirror* was, surprisingly, the most substantial. The reporter who conducted it was, as it happened, a guitar enthusiast and he did his work with great respect – and without any trace of 'tabloidery.' Afterwards he told me that, although he had interviewed countless people, many of them VIPs of one kind or another, and had been a journalist for many years, it was the first time he had felt that he was not controlling the interview; there was no pejorative overtone in this statement! He said also that he too had known by some sort of alchemy when the moment had come for him to make his exit – another new experience for him.

ELDER STATESMAN

In his last decades Segovia was the undisputed Elder States-
man (The 'Pope,' as he was wont to describe himself) of the classic
guitar, the father figure and oracle to whom younger players
turned for advice and guidance, and he carried the regalia of his
office with dignity, as to the manner born, receiving all and sundry
with benevolence and courtesy. Those who met with his approval
were often given a helping hand, usually in the form of a written
reference and, in exceptional cases, by commending the benefi-
ciary to the attention of his agents. I never asked him to document
his approval of my own work, nor did he ever volunteer to do so
(except in the case of my *Foundation studies in classic guitar
technique*), but the situation of a composer is different from that
of a performer. Instead, he signalled his approval by telling people
all over the world that I wrote good music for the guitar (confirmed to me by many of those to whom he said this) and, more
importantly, by playing and recording some of my work. In his
early years Segovia persuaded composers to write for him by
displaying his artistry as an object worthy of their attention; he
did not have the money to offer them financial inducement. As he
became successful and famous the situation changed: he no longer
needed to prove his artistry, nor did he need to offer money. A
composer's payment came in the form of status, in that his works
were played by Segovia, and substantial financial reward through
performance and recording royalties. He knew as well as anyone
that composers, like the rest of mankind, need money to meet
their obligations, and that 'the laborer is worthy of his hire'; he
knew also that some payments may also be liberally made
'in kind.'

Chapter Six

Guitars were another matter. The story has often been told of the guitar given by Ramirez to Segovia, then 18 years old and near the beginning of his career, but this did not set the pattern for later years. There may have been other, later freebies but at some point he decided that there would be no more – though right up to the time of his death there can have been few luthiers who would not gladly have given him their best instruments, whether for professional gratification or status (= concomitant profit). In the early 1960s he told me that he never accepted a guitar as a gift from any luthier, because he felt that it would have placed him under some obligation to use it, which he might not always have wished to fulfil. In this connection he mentioned a guitar he had bought some years previously from a well-known European luthier, which had failed to live up to the early promise that had induced him to buy it. Every time they re-met, the luthier asked about his instrument – and was told: "The molecules [of the wood] have not yet settled down." They never did.

THE MESSIANIC FACTOR

In one way World War II was a watershed in Segovia's career. He had by then achieved considerable fame and had made a number of gramophone records, but the guitar remained entirely outside the mainstream of serious music-making; also, it was identified in the mind of the musical public with the name of Segovia. His stated objectives of winning unqualified recognition for the guitar as a 'standard' musical instrument, and of introducing it into tertiary musical education must still have seemed far-distant. Whether they have even now been accomplished remains debatable, but that is beside our immediate point.

No doubt he was aware of the fragility of the guitar's and his own position, and conscious of how easily the hard-won ground might be lost. Failure would have been severely damaging to the future of the instrument – and, no less, to his self-esteem; the road he had taken would have ended abruptly over a cliff. He was convinced that this road was the right and only one, as he remained for the rest of his days, and that it was his personal mission to follow it, taking the guitar with him. Just as the lute was not to be permitted to cloud the instrumental issue, other living guitarists posed potential threats to his position as the guitar's mentor, especially those whose technical and (less) musical approaches differed from his own – and therefore from those which he saw as vital to the instrument's well-being.

He did not, so far as I know, write a testimonial letter for any other player before World War II. This was certainly not because there was no-one who was worthy of his support. In 1967 he wrote feelingly, glowingly, and no doubt sincerely [30] about the recently deceased Ida Presti, but, though he had heard her play when she was young (and surviving recordings testify to the magnificence of her playing when she was only 14), he withheld his help at a time when it would have been invaluable to her. Although she remained profoundly respectful of Segovia and his contribution, she was privately saddened by his lack of early support. He described another famous guitarist of the time as: "A marvellous machine, but without a mechanic!" – although he/she played in much the same romantic vein as Segovia himself, albeit with his/her own particular and different brand of that persuasive warmth that comes from the heart that loved music and the guitar with passion.

His trench-warfare with Emilio Pujol, who opposed the use of the right-hand nails, was undisguised, and as a celebrated academic Pujol had a status that made him a doubly dangerous 'opponent.' Pujol's mildness of manner, not to mention his far lower profile as a concert artist, prevented him from militant involvement in the battle, but he remained as totally convinced of his own rightness as Segovia was of his own. He was, however, not above petulance: Ida Presti had, after trying it, abandoned the no-nails technique and this rankled with Pujol. When in the late 1960s a friend of mine mentioned Presti to Pujol he affected at first not to recognize the name but, when pressed, finally said "Oh – the French woman." In 1967, when I guest-edited the memorial issue of *Guitar Review*, dedicated to Presti, [31] I wrote to Pujol to ask if he would write an article on guitar duos to include in it. He politely declined, saying that he was too busy, but he did not offer to pen a few words of appreciation of Presti herself – which would have taken little more time than it took to write his letter of reply!

Segovia was reluctant to help others with their performing careers between the two wars, though he was not entirely inflexible in some cases, as in the following one – of which he himself told me. When he felt that he had been 'bent' too far, he snapped! A less famous guitarist of his acquaintance (we will call him A.B.) wrote to him, saying that he was scheduled to play a recital in a European city within a very short time of one to be given by Segovia, which, Segovia being who he was, would inevitably take its toll of his own audience. Therefore, would Segovia be so kind and friendly as to consider cancelling his concert, one which was far less important to him than A.B's was to him? Segovia replied, that he had tried to do so but had been told by the promoters that it was too late; all the seats had been sold. This provoked a testy response, A.B. complaining of Segovia's lack of generosity and consideration for a less-famous artist, which in turn triggered the final salvo in the affair: "My dear A. I have done everything in my power to help you, but the one thing I cannot do is to give you the necessary *talent.*"

The years following World War II brought developments that were important to Segovia. Air-travel, boosted by the advent of the jet engine, expanded greatly and it became easier and quicker for a concert artist to circle the earth, wasting less time in travelling from one country or venue to another by surface transport. The gramophone industry also expanded rapidly, and music (and therefore those who produced it) entered more homes than ever before, in larger 'units' and with greatly improved sound-quality when the long-playing record reached the market place in the late 1940s. Not long after this, the guitar in all its forms floated on the crest of a wave of popularity, multiplying the number of those 'sinners' who were in need of a 'Pope.' The music schools, colleges and academies began to appoint 'professors' or tutors of the guitar. Within a decade the guitar's world prospered, Segovia's dreams seemed to be coming true, and he was the unchallenged monarch of the realm. By now his doubts and fears, even his latent sense of insecurity, must have been abated – though they were perhaps too chronically ingrained to disappear completely. The optimistic epithet 'the next Segovia' had for long been affixed to many young and 'promising' guitarists but now, within sight of his 'promised land,' Segovia himself clearly felt secure and benevolent enough to bestow his own honors. Their first recipient might chronologically have been Julian Bream but in the event it was John Williams, receiving the honorary princedom that understandably featured in his earlier promotional material. Williams was the first of many, though the only one to be described in such regal terms, and there are now many such letters of commendation in the world, some of those later bestowed suggestive of surprisingly liberal judgment.

SENSE OF HUMOR

Segovia was famous as a guitarist and musician, and almost equally so as a raconteur with a seemingly inexhaustible fund of anecdotes, with which he could lubricate any difficult social interface. They tended to grow out of the prevailing line of conversation, rather than randomly recalled to fill lacunæ, and it must inevitably have been impossible for him to remember which ones he had told to whom, so that over the years there were many that one heard several times – some of which have been remembered in print by other writers: I have tried to avoid repeating these. Some others were told to me only once, and in this connection I now regret having refrained from recording our conversations, for there are many that are now lost to the memory. Although many of his anecdotes were humorous in a general way, some enshrined jokes at other people's expense; though this must be true of most of us, I never heard him tell a story in which he lost the encounter. The taste for telling jokes against oneself is perhaps associated with certain nationalities rather than others, but the absence of it can also be consistent with a desire not to appear vulnerable – a mark of ego or insecurity, or even both. Four small examples stay green in my memory; each told with a twinkle in the eye:

(1) A gathering of guitar people had been wide-eyed (and -eared) at the spectacle of a famous flamenco player's digital pyrotechnics. Segovia took a guitar and executed the 'famous' exercise in chromatic octaves in the nut position at considerable speed, after

which the flamenco wizard, taking the bait, tried in vain to do likewise, thereby losing face. This is consistent with Segovia's lack of respect for speed per se: on one occasion I played a record of a guitar duo (not Presti-Lagoya!) which seriously challenged the land-speed record; afterwards he said: "It is very clever – but who wants to listen to a man talking fast all the time?"

(2) When Pablo Casals, aged 80, married his young student, aged 20, Segovia sent him a telegram: "My dear Pablo, I do congratulate you, but you should remember that you are eighty years old – and not four times twenty!" If Pablo Casals returned the compliment when Segovia married Emilita, I never heard about it; even had the mathematics been amenable, which they were not, the joke would have been second-hand.

(3) One evening Segovia dined with a family of some social distinction. After dinner the daughter of the family, whose assets did not include physical attractiveness, played the guitar to him – very badly. Such a situation was by no means unfamiliar to Segovia, who had a generous stock of phrases with which simultaneously to avoid saying neither what he did not mean nor what he really thought. Had he pointed his life in a different direction he might have become an asset to the diplomatic service. However, on this occasion the situation was made more difficult when, as he left, the young lady requested him to sign her autograph book. This he did: "To my dear....., whose beauty is equalled only by that of her guitar playing."

(4) After listening to John Williams' recording of my *Variations on a Catalan folk-song*, he said: "I congratulate the player. I congratulate the recording company. I congratulate the guitar and the

strings" – and, after an impish pause, "and I congratulate
the composer!"

ANGLOPHILIA

It is perhaps surprising to find acute Anglophilia in a loyal
Spaniard but Segovia did in fact 'suffer' from this amiable condition. If he had not been born a Spaniard, which he was eternally
grateful to have been, I am sure that he would have liked to have
been British. Rarely were his visits to London mere minimal
'frames' for his recitals; their length proclaimed his simple love of
being there. My *English Suite* sprang from his affection for British
folk music, a response to his request that I should adapt some of it
to the guitar. It was not, however, only British *music* that he
loved, as two small anecdotes make clear. His marriage to Emilita
took place in Gibraltar and he explained this to me thus: "In order
that we might be married under the British flag, on Spanish soil."
When the birth of Carlos Andrés was imminent he brought
Emilita to London in order that the event might take place there:
"Because in England is the best ante- and post-natal care in the
world...and so that Carlos Andrés may have the option of retaining
or rejecting a British passport." He later repaid the 'favor' by
devoting the entire proceeds of a recital in the Royal Festival Hall
to the Hospital and to gynæcological research. This typically
generous act mirrored earlier ones: the London Royal College of
Music benefited similarly from his recital there on 8 May 1962, as
did St. Mary's Hospital (London) on 13 May 1963.

THE SHORT FUSE

A very 'Mediterranean' trait in Segovia's character was the
quickness of his temper, which could blow up suddenly and
fiercely – and subside just as abruptly. When he was in Manches-

ter in 1949 he invited Terry Usher and I to watch him practice in his hotel room. At that time Terry was obsessively interested in the 'geometrical' and 'photographic' aspects of playing technique and, in order to get a worm's-eye view of Segovia's right hand in action, he crawled in front of him on all fours and peered up, along the line of the strings. Segovia was looking to his left at the time but, his peripheral vision maybe detecting some unscheduled movement, he looked to his right – and saw Terry's rapt face just above floor level; his eyebrows elevated and his eyes widened a little but he said nothing. Shortly after that the phone rang and on answering it his mood changed: he was *furious* and after a few minutes of verbal red-heat he slammed the receiver down, picked it up again and told the operator not to put through any further call until he sanctioned it. But it rang again almost immediately and it was obviously the same caller. This time his rage was awe-inspiring to behold. Our almost total ignorance of Spanish, the language with which the battle was being fought, prevented us from grasping anything of the substance of the bone of contention, but this was unimportant – and of course none of our business; here was a vision of a man in transports of rage such as we had never before witnessed in real life, and we could only admire his verbal agility in negotiating streams of bubbling labials – rather like the sound of a wine bottle being emptied under high pressure. Finally the receiver was slammed down and was not lifted again during our visit. Immediately his mood changed back to one of easy amiability, as if at the press of a switch. We knew who had been at the other end of the line, but we never did find out what had caused the explosion.

In teaching of *any* kind it is usual for the master to issue instruction of one sort or another; it is, or should be, equally commonplace for the student to ask for clarification – to ask the 'why?' that explains the 'what.' Such does not seem always to have been the case in Segovia's master classes, where to ask 'why?' was to take one's life in one's hands. Two of my friends experienced this at first hand when, having asked the hazardous question, they were imperiously dismissed to the outer darkness. A few years after these passages of arms I mentioned them to Segovia, explaining that those concerned were neither challenging his authority nor questioning the validity of what he had told them; they only wanted to understand the basic principles behind the directives, so that they could apply them in other contexts. He unquestioningly accepted my explanations and told me to tell the 'exiles' not to hesitate to come to see him at any future time – all was forgiven. I passed on the information but I do not know whether any reconciliation ever took place. What is interesting here is the *extremeness* of Segovia's original reaction to what most others would have regarded as a fair and reasonable question. It suggests that, at least, he was unversed in the basics of ordinary teaching, a two-way process, as opposed to the authoritarian master class situation to which he was accustomed. He did not hear 'why?' as a contraction of 'I am only a student and I do not for a moment question the rightness of what you, the great Segovia, have told me; I would simply like to *understand* what it is founded on, so that I may make use of it in the future"; what he heard was a challenge to his authority. Was this another symptom of lurking insecurity, maybe a fear that he could not always give a logical answer because so much that he did was instinctive? I have witnessed like situations in classes given by some of today's most famous players, whose reactions have differed diametrically from Segovia's. They either give reasons or, occasionally, admit their inability to do so – a physical action may be something which they have found empirically to be suited to themselves, or a musical point merely reflects how they *feel* about it, but in neither case can they approach the matter in a general analytical way. I often asked Segovia 'why?' and always received a calm answer, if not always (as with the use of F♯ tuning!) an entirely convincing one, but I was not in a public, master/student relationship with him, and he could not in any case have regarded me as an incipient performer who might be tilting at his authority. The difference was probably of key-significance.

In his relationship with critics he was no less hypersensitive and, like many other artists, ambivalent. Once, after reading a mildly adverse review, he said to me: "What *are* these critics? They are *nothing* without their newspapers" – which is of course often far from the truth. However, his agents carefully assembled every published review and either showed or sent them all on to him; I have no reason to believe that he did not scrutinise them all. It was not necessary for a critic to write an adverse review in order to incur his wrath, as an occasion in the early 1970s demonstrated. After a Royal Festival Hall recital no newspaper published a review. He vented his rage on (but not at) me; mine were probably the first suitable ears to be available. "Never again," he proclaimed, would he "play in a city whose press could behave in this way," ignoring the presence of a major artist. Once again I found myself in the role of counsel for the defense, explaining that there were so many concerts on any one night in London, and that it was impossible for any newspaper to maintain enough critics, or find page-space to review them all – and there was perhaps some justice in devoting what space there was to helping up-and-coming artists, to whom publicity was far more important than it was to him. Again he accepted what I said, but I do not for one moment imagine that this played any part in persuading him to return – as he did, many times. It was just another of those flash storms that was bound to subside when reason supplanted rage; I cannot believe that he ever had any serious intention to boycott the London scene!

LOYALTY

An essential feature of his character was his loyalty to those he regarded as true friends, for whom he would do anything within his power. Though he was given to harboring grudges, he never forgot the help and friendship he received from others. An archetypal case was that of Torroba, the first to respond to his pleas in the 1920s for new works. One day, shortly after he had received the score of Torroba's *Castles of Spain*, he showed me a deep pile of music he had earmarked for attention; he said that because Torroba had placed *him* first, all those years ago, he would always give top priority to anything he wrote for him. The pile of other scores would have to wait until Torroba's castles were explored. His loyalty to Torroba was not just a simple *quid pro quo*, it was warmed with a real affection. One evening in November 1981, after dinner, I asked if he had heard Pepe Romero's recording of Torroba's *Diálogos* (in my opinion, one of the very finest of all recorded works for guitar and orchestra). He had not. The work was in fact intended (by Torroba) to be performed by Segovia at his own farewell concert, an event which of course never took place, nor was ever likely to have done – and the piece was in any case too difficult for Segovia to handle at that stage. Not only had he not heard Pepe's recording, he had never even *heard* the piece, so I played the record to him. He sat on the front of his chair in rapt attention. One movement of the work is based on Torroba's *Romance de los pinos*, a piece which Segovia often played as the valedictory encore to his recitals, 'good night' becoming 'farewell.' At the end, whilst commenting on the masterly performance, Segovia took out his handkerchief and mopped his eyes. It was a moving moment – and not only for him.

In a different connection, speaking to a young guitar duo who were on the threshold of their career – and considering changing their British agent, he advised them to weather it out with one agent and not to indulge in 'agent-shopping.' You must, he said, build up a long-standing working relationship and trust with an agent, and be patient. He cited examples of his own long associations, including that with Ibbs and Tillett, which agency he had joined when the late Emmie Tillett, for many years its director, was just Mr. Tillett's secretary. Segovia outlived Mrs. Tillett (as he did so many of those with whom he enjoyed long associations!) and remained with the agency until the time of his death. Though this was probably sound advice, I am not sure that he fully understood the difference between the two situations: that of the young, upwardly mobile Andrés Segovia in the interim years between the two World Wars, and that of two young, married players who were struggling to make headway in the more competitive world of the 1970s. The two were hardly comparable.

DISLIKE OF THE SUBSTANDARD

Segovia was a severely quality-first man. It was primarily important to him that a thing should be well done, in accordance with what is good in the human spirit as he perceived it, whether the thing be simple or complex. In short, he had a clearly defined scale of values which he applied to everything and to all situations. If some of his actions seem to contradict this we should remember that as a mortal he was fallible, and as liable as most of us to lose sight of his new-year resolutions when provoked; an exceptionally long life-span provides correspondingly more opportunities for this! In the everyday things his tastes were uncomplicated: good food, simply but well prepared – a tender steak or a piece of fish (especially turbot) was a sure-fire winner, good wine (seldom more than one glass), clothes that were unpretentious but superbly tailored (he went to high-class West End tailors for his dress suits [32]) and good conversation. On the Big Occasion he could 'put on the Ritz' with the best of them, but, like his dress at such times, it represented only his formal exterior.

Contact with other people demanded courtesy and it was always forthcoming, no matter how tired or harassed he felt. Only when he met extreme discourtesy in others did he exercise his formidable talent for crushing the opposition, not by being discourteous but by directing a well-aimed barb at the heart of the offense. His dislike of what he regarded as substandard was not restricted to musical works and their interpretations, and to what he considered to be improper on-stage deportment – to which I have referred elsewhere. Some 20 years ago he raged against someone who had published an arrangement of a Sonata of Scarlatti, of which he himself had published one many years before, using a term that, had it been pronounced in public, might have provoked legal action. The 'offender' had in fact not used Segovia's arrangement as his 'Ursprung' but had worked from the original score, avoiding some errors in Segovia's text in the process! This is a very shadowy area: some kind of 'precedence' must attach to whomever first produces the first arrangement of a particular piece in a particular key; the idea was his/hers. But the Law does not confer automatic exclusivity: how much an arrangement must be different, and in what ways, from one that is already in print before it escapes from a legally provable charge of plagiary, is far from clear. As the Law does not supply clear-cut answers we must depend on the honesty of authors who produce such second versions; that this is equally unreliable is shown by the many published arrangements that are shamelessly derived directly from pre-existing ones by others. Today we have to learn to live with this shabby situation but we may perhaps sympathize with the feelings of a man, Segovia, who became – though not by choice – the 'foster father' of so many such 'children of dubious legitimacy.' There can, of course, be no valid objection to 'second' editions which, through the exercise of scholarship, significantly improve an earlier one or correct significant errors in it.

Failure to maintain what he regarded as high standards in important matters provoked a wrath from which no-one was immune. A small peccadillo might soon have been forgiven (though placed 'on file') but a larger one, as he saw it, would incur longer-lasting fury. When a famous guitarist became over-catholic in his activities, making forays 'across the tracks,' Segovia was beside himself with rage; as the person concerned was one to whom he had previously given unstinting support, the *volte face* must have caused Segovia some agonizing heart-searching. Some time before a competition in which Segovia was to be the president of the jury, the proposal that the offending artist should be a member of the jury was not well received. He said to me: "He (the offender) has betrayed the guitar; he has undermined everything I have ever tried to do. I have told the organizers that they may choose: they may have either him or me – I will not sit in the same room as this man." Much later, however, he showed signs of coming to terms with the situation; referring to it, he said:

"Maybe such things are not regarded so seriously in other places as they are in Spain." But the breach never mended!

ATTITUDE TO OLD AGE

To anyone concerned with the guitar, Segovia seemed to be immortal. Only the very old could remember a time when he was not there, the personification of the classic guitar, and it was difficult to imagine a world from which he would be absent – though such a thing was occasionally mooted in an abstract way. That he was becoming significantly 'old' was obvious in many ways but it still did not seem that there would ever be a definitive end to the process.

In the course of his/her performing life an artist follows two lines. The first represents the growth of wisdom, maturity and sensitivity with increasing age; this process continues on a rising curve, unless it be arrested by senility. The second is a parabola: technical mastery may grow with time, but at some point it reaches its apogee and thereafter, aided by less reliable memory, diminishes as age takes its inevitable physical toll. The two curves reinforce one another until the parabola begins its downward path, marking the end of the artist's 'golden age,' and once this separation becomes evident the listener must increasingly focus on the musical artistry and make ever-greater allowances for the decay of technique.

My own assessment is that Segovia's golden years were those of his fifties and sixties, and that as he entered his seventies it became obvious that the two curves were beginning to go their separate ways. In one year he would give a Royal Festival Hall recital that was ridden with slips and forgettings, in which it was patent that he was far from being at ease; one thought that this marked the end of the road, the beginning of a short path to retirement. Then, in the next, he would return to give a performance of such quality that the previous year's seemed maybe to be a false alarm, a passing aberration – until the next year, when the danger signals were again hoisted for all to see and hear. The process of alternation went on for some years, but it petered out with his seventies and we were left to savor the somewhat sporadic moments of untrammelled beauty and, for the rest, to remember how it had once been. A few years before the end, he temporarily transferred his patronage to the new Barbican Hall (he told me that the Royal Festival had become too expensive) where on one occasion the situation was encapsulated in a brief conversation I had with an enthusiast, who had travelled up from the north country to hear Segovia. Whilst recognizing that the technique had fallen into ruin, he said: "But it doesn't matter. Even if he'd just walked on, bowed, and walked off, carrying his guitar, it would have been worth it!" Such was the thrall in which Segovia held his admirers, that of gratitude for what he had done, rather than realistic admiration for what he was by then actually *doing*.

A performing artist reaches the public in two basic ways: through live performances and through recordings, of which the latter are the more important in the long run, continuing to represent the player even after his/her death – composers are more fortunate in this respect! Today's leading virtuosi enjoy the benefit of the synergetic effect of concert appearances and a plethora of recordings, as did Segovia – until the 1970s. What happened then was told to me by Segovia himself, and confirmed by English Decca executives at that time. His recording contract had been with the parent company in the U.S.A., which was then adopting the policy of making no further recordings of classical music. The company is however a subsidiary of the giant Music Corporation of America (MCA), which, as the 1970s dawned, decided to establish their own base in Britain, promoting their own (MCA) record label. To this end they set up shop in London, appropriated and deleted all the existing recordings by Segovia (and others) and proceeded to re-issue them on the MCA label with new album-titles, the crassest of which was "El Fabuloso." I do not know what commercial target they set for the operation; whatever it was, they appear not to have reached it. The London tent was folded and the recordings that had not been reissued were replaced in Decca's lap. Whilst Decca UK were able to sell the residual stocks of the revamped albums, they could not press more of them, nor could they re-issue the remainder as 'new' recordings. The only course that was open was to offer them all as budget-price reissues, from which Segovia would receive correspondingly smaller royalties; this he was not prepared to accept. The net result was the disappearance of so many of his recordings from the market, leaving a gap that still remains. Segovia made several more recordings for RCA in Spain but only one of these was released in Britain; they were, moreover, made at a time when the decline of his technical facility was already patent – as reflected in the title of the UK-released album "Reveries." [31] The tragedy was not so much that the flow of new recordings ceased, but that the important, formerly available ones vanished from the market place. It was 1980 before the HMV recordings made between 1927-1939 were reissued on long-playing records (they are now available also on compact discs [32] and even now there must be many thousands of guitar *aficionados* who neither possess nor have heard them. As a result there are generations of guitarists whose experience of his playing has been more or less confined to that which they heard in the live recitals of his autumnal/winter years.

To these people he became a 'legend,' to be revered for what he had done, but with some reservation – 'No doubt he was wonderful in his day, but time has marched on and standards have risen. Today's virtuosi, with their precision-engineered techniques and fleet fingers, show just how far we have travelled since the time when Segovia was considered to be so remarkable.' Had the evidence of those deleted recordings continued to be freely available it would have shown the error of such an assessment, no matter how understandably formed. Big Business has much to answer for, though in this case I doubt that it cares overly, but it must be admitted that in his proud refusal to enter the bargain basement Segovia scored an 'own goal.' The loss was not only his; it is shared by later generations who were thus deprived of access to these important archives.

Why did he continue to tour for so long after it was clear to everyone (including, I am sure, himself) that his performances were for the most part 'ghosts of Christmas past'? I believe there were several reasons, but two will suffice. Since 1909 his life had become filled with concert tours, relieved only by rest periods during the summer months. The rest was primarily from his 'life on the road,' for daily practice had to continue, new pieces had to be assimilated and old ones refurbished, and a programme had to be put together for the next tour and/or recording. In his old age he leaned much more heavily (at the end, entirely) on refurbishment, and learned little new repertoire – and certainly nothing that was too taxing on his energies and memory; by then even such small gains must have been hard-won. The main frame of his life was however the concert-giving, the touring that took him to old and new places, and enabled him to renew friendships. To those things to which we become accustomed as essentials of life – breathing, eating, drinking and sleeping, he added the round of travelling, playing, the prospect of full auditoria, standing ovations, and the life-enhancing participation in the world of the guitar and music, to which he had so single-mindedly devoted himself. Had he retired it was, in the view of many of his close friends, unlikely that he would have lived long. When that first September in retirement arrived and he realized that there was to be no more touring, that the reward of audience-response would be only a memory – and maybe felt that people no longer *needed* him, the effect would have been utterly devastating. His concert career lasted for more than 77 years, one of the longest in the history of music, and like any other long-standing 'habit,' it would have been punishingly difficult to bring to an abrupt end – 'cold turkey' indeed. One day in 1976 Alexandre Tansman commented to me that: "If Andrés ever retires from playing, he will be dead in six months." Estimates by other old friends ranged from three months to two years, but in essence they were unanimous. In the end they were irrelevant, for he never actually retired.

He himself gave another reason for his persistence in his oft-quoted: "I will retire when my public retires from me." This sounded like a formula for an undignified end to a great career, a whimper to which few would be listening, but I doubt that he regarded it as a serious possibility. In the course of a private conversation in 1980 he said to me: "All over the world I am playing in halls that are full of people – who think that they may be seeing me for the last time!" This was certainly true, though there were many who stayed away because they preferred to remember him as he was in his best years, it remained true for the rest of his life, and it seems unlikely that it would ever have changed; had his playing declined to the point at which people were not prepared to come even to 'pay homage' he would surely have known it and would have spared everyone, including himself, such embarrassment. In short, one answer to the question: 'Why did he continue for so long?' was the counter-question: "Why not?" As long as people were prepared to flock to hear him, whilst knowing well what to expect, why should he not have played for them? Another great performer, in the last years of whose career age took its toll, was Artur Rubinstein; he remarked (I paraphrase): "The critics always write about the wrong notes I play. Why don't they ever say anything about the ones I get right?" Those who had known Segovia's playing in his best years either returned to be reminded of earlier, golden times, and to pay their respects, or preferred to keep it green in the memory; those who had not, came to witness the personage of a living legend (maybe for that 'last time') and to be able to say: "I was *there*." Different strokes for different folks.

Segovia was very much aware of his advancing years. In a letter I wrote to him sometime in the 1960s, over a quarter of a century before his life ended, I mentioned that in England we called him 'the old man.' His reply was: "My young wife is sitting by me and she says that she cannot see an old man." I reassured him that we use the term to describe the 'boss,' as for example the captain of a ship, and that it does not refer to cardinal age; the 'old man' may be still in his twenties – if he has already acquired the necessary status! He accepted my explanation gratefully. During the same decade I once asked him if he still adhered to his daily practice routine: "Yes, now more than ever. When I was young, if I made a mistake people would say: 'Ah, last night he was drinking – or with a woman'; but *now*, if I make mistakes, they say it is because I am growing old!" On another occasion when we were together in his hotel room he excused himself, saying: "Now I must practice. When you do not practice alone it is like taking your clothes off in front of a stranger." He had clearly forgotten the occasion in 1949 when he *invited* Terry and I to watch him doing so, but he was then a youthful fifty-six, not a 'vulnerable' seventy-plus!

As one ages, physical things become more difficult – hills get steeper, objects grow heavier, and the body responds more grudgingly; one becomes aware that it is harder (and ultimately impossible) to play a musical instrument with the security and fluency of youth. In his last decades this must have been very apparent to Segovia. He never spoke to me of it but it became manifest in his growing dissatisfaction with his tools. Entering his hotel room I was often confronted with a coffee table, groaning under the weight of discarded strings (especially the monofils) and empty packets, a veritable graveyard of nylon filaments. When one thinks of the sheer physical effort of putting on and taking off so many strings, it is not difficult to imagine its effect on his patience and morale! He was unable to find a satisfactory string (most usually the first) and, if he had not already done so, was about to cable to New York to request the dispatch by express mail of a batch of hand-picked strings; sometimes they had already arrived and were also to be found on the coffee table. On at least one occasion he went on-stage with a second string doing duty for a first! There is little doubt that string-making is not quite what it was when bass strings were individually wound by hand, a process that became no longer economically viable; every performer has his/her own tales of woe to tell – my own favorite is that of one of my students who found the octave harmonic on a brand-new first string of a very famous mark to be located at the *fourteenth* fret!

However it is a common affliction, with which players must learn to live and to solve it as best they can. To Segovia it became, in his old age, a means of attributing at least some of his technical problems to external factors, as opposed to the toll that was being exacted by his advancing years. Several times he greeted us in the green room after a recital with: "Did you hear what that string [or sometimes "guitar"] *did* to me?!" It was a very human foible, and one that lies in wait for all of us when age robs us of flexible youth's capacity to override such obstacles, taking them in its stride: This conviction, that a recital had become a battle against his strings or even the guitar itself, must have disturbed his concentration and further strained his memory. One of the notable features of his recitals had always been the nimble way in which he corrected the pitch of errant strings in midstream, using a fleetingly disengaged hand to turn the tuning peg; in this his efforts became fewer and less effective in his last years.

All this must have imposed tremendous strain on Segovia, trying his best to live up to his monumental reputation – with steadily diminishing resources. It was painfully evident after his recital in the Avery Fisher Hall in New York in February 1974. The recital had not gone well. At one point in the *Tarantella* of Castelnuovo-Tedesco his memory failed utterly and, after a few fruitless efforts to regain control, he played the final cadence. Respectfully, the audience began to applaud but it was silenced; Segovia sat rigidly in place with a grim expression and raised his right hand with a commanding gesture, like that of a policeman bringing the traffic to a halt. He recommenced and, with a brief moment of cliff-hanging at the previous trouble-spot, saw the piece safely to its end. After the recital my wife and I went to the green-room door, fighting our way through what W.C. Fields might have described as "a solid wall of human flesh," and found it tight-shut. Persistent knocking, finally provoked the appearance of a guardian of the gate, to whom we gave our names; after consultation with the powers within he admitted us. Only about one dozen people were allowed in – and the reason was soon obvious. Segovia sat (a thing he had very rarely done at such times) behind a small table, looking totally drained; his speech was slow and uncharacteristically lack-lustre, though he was signing programmes in his usual, gracious fashion. When our turn came he looked at me blankly (he had no idea that we were in New York – and it was the first time he had seen me with the beard I had acquired that January) and after several seconds he said: "You are concealed; you are like Solzhenitsin!" We were to see him many more times in a similar condition, though his managers did not always have the good sense and consideration to provide him with a seat.

When Emilita began to travel with him she assumed responsibility for many of the day-to-day chores, those things to which a road manager might normally attend to, but which Segovia himself had previously dealt with. He became accustomed to this, and in his last years dependent upon it. When he was in his early nineties, and travelling alone, he telephoned to me on the morning after his London recital: "Can you tell me where I am supposed to go next?" I was reminded of the English writer who, accompanied by his famously unreliable memory, was on tour; he cabled to his secretary in London: "I am in Birmingham. Where *should* I be?" – but it was sad to find him in this sorry state, one which a few years earlier would have been unimaginable. On his last tours in Britain he was accompanied by a professional road manager who relieved him of any such problem. It was at this same stage of his life that he once began a telephone call to me in French, a thing he had never done before because of the difference between our accents; I answered in the same language and it remained thus throughout the rest of the conversation. Strangely, neither of us had any apparent difficulty! In a conversation not long before his ninetieth year he uttered the heart-cry: "It is tragic that now, in the autumn of my career and near the end of my life, I cannot get satisfactory strings or a good guitar." This, from a man who had known and survived the traumas of living with gut and silk strings! But it was not so much the autumn as the winter.

HEALTH

Comparatively few have the good fortune to reach their ninety-fifth year without having fallen victim to some incapacitating ailment well before then, especially those approaching the end of a physically punishing life on the treadmill of constant touring. I have never met any young artist who has expressed the wish to emulate this aspect of Segovia's life; many have declared the contrary. Nor of course do the most successful now *need* to continue for longer than they really wish: modern facilities for travel and propagation via recorded sound enable an artist to 'compress' his/her career, achieving the same fame and fortune in far less time and/or with less physical effort. Up to the time of his death Segovia was still mobile, albeit with the aid of a walking stick, his eyesight did not appear to be all that much worse than it had been for many years before then, and his mental faculties were still sharp – though his responses were noticeably slower and it was more difficult than it had been to conduct a steadily focused conversation with him, a problem to which deafness in his left ear contributed. He could not however have survived such a long and hard-working life had he not been blessed with a remarkably strong constitution. In the late 1950s he told me that he had only twice ever had to cancel a recital through indisposition – and that in one case he had recovered by the due date, and could have played had the recital not been cancelled as a precaution. At about the same time I discussed the matter with one Alex Martinez, a Spanish-born doctor who had been a boyhood companion of Segovia; I first met him in Liverpool in the 1930s, but he was by then living near Clapham Common. He said: "Andrés is like every other male Spaniard – a hypochondriac!" He said that when Segovia travelled alone he would sometimes telephone to him (often in the small hours of the morning) to say that he was very ill – and "please come to see me immediately." When he did he found him in perfectly good shape, needing nothing more than reassurance or a placebo. "The truth is that he's as healthy as a horse!" was Alex's summation. The truth is, also, that Segovia suffered no small amount in his working life: an operation to rectify displaced retinas in the 1950s might have resulted in blindness (which he knew before it was carried out) but happily did not, and later, more painful ones included treatment for hernia and gallstones. Toward the end of his life he suffered from gout, and one evening I entered his hotel room to find him sock-less and with his trousers rolled up, his feet immersed in a basin of warm water. Sometime in the 1960s he told me that he was a chronic insomniac and asked if I knew of any remedy; I suggested a few that I had found variously effective, but he never mentioned the matter again.

That he was able to continue in the face of these misfortunes, and to show little or nothing of them to his public, was owed to his incredibly strong constitution – and to his determination not to be beaten. I do not think he feared death – but, as he loved what he was doing on earth, he wished to avoid it for as long as possible. When he was asked in a television interview how he looked on the prospect of the hereafter he said: "God, I know that Your Heaven is a wonderful place, but I am a miserable sinner who does not deserve to enter it: please leave me where I am!" At various times he described himself as a "confused" or "distracted" Catholic, but in one conversation, when I had mentioned that my own belief was non-denominational, he said: "We are both believers. When you consider the beauty and the complexity of the Universe you know that *Someone* must have created it; you *must* be a believer."

LATE RENAISSANCE

There was no doubting that his marriage to Emilita, his third and last wife, rejuvenated him. Just as one's game of golf is raised when one is with a much better player, one recovers some of one's distant youth when one associates with someone who is much younger. His second 'renaissance' came with the birth of their son Carlos Andrés in 1970. Although fatherhood was by no means a novel experience to him (he had had three other children, of whom only one had survived – another Andrés, a successful painter who lives in Paris) his enthusiasm for it remained un-dimmed despite (or maybe because of) his age – 77 at the time! Thereafter his visits brought the familiar baby pictures, proudly extracted from his wallet, reports on progress and the inevitable anecdotes. One of these last dated from the time at which Carlos Andrés had become erectly mobile and articulate, on an occasion when he remained in Spain with Emilita while his father was on tour. He listened intently to one of Segovia's records; when the music stopped he walked round to the back of one of the floor-standing loudspeakers and said: "Daddy, come out!" That the imposing figure of Andrés Segovia (complete with guitar) might even be compressed into, let alone function within, a domestic loudspeaker, is a notion that could inhabit only the fertile imagination of a small child

REMINISCENCES

A full account of Segovia's experiences during a long and active life that spanned the years of the guitar's 20th-century revival could have had unique archival value; it was begun but never completed. The first installment of his autobiography, entitled "*La guitarra y yo*" (The guitar and myself) appeared in the fourth issue of the New York *Guitar Review* (1947) but the series petered out, at an early stage in the story, in the thirteenth issue (1952); its discontinuation was not explained but it may have been due to the fact that his career was then expanding rapidly and he simply lacked the time. A necessarily brief summary of his life preserved the sound of his voice for posterity in two recordings, on the Decca label and bearing the same title as the previous, written account. [35] After that he addressed himself seriously to the task of writing his integral autobiography, the first volume of which (1893-1920) was published in 1976 (Macmillan, New York), appearing one year later in a British edition (Marion Boyars, London). It was dedicated "to my son Carlos Andrés."

There were obvious difficulties in confronting a task of these dimensions – to recall a career of such long duration, at so late a stage in life, when the remaining years might be regarded as 'borrowed time' and one is in the natural course of things working more and more slowly, and hampered by deteriorating eyesight. Memory becomes increasingly unreliable and capricious: the good tends to be superlatively upgraded, the bad may be 'Freudianly' forgotten or even consciously passed over, because one wishes to leave as good an impression as possible. When an autobiography reaches those years that were shared by many others who are still alive, it may involve the recording of value-judgments or honest opinions that might prove embarrassing to their subjects or their close kin (for which reason I omit from this book certain of the comments Segovia made to me), and any distortion of the facts (whether wilful or through simple waywardness of memory) is liable to be challenged by others whose recollection of them is different. Even when the facts are undeniable and the opinions are utterly sincere, relationships may become strained – or even destroyed, when one might wish to keep them amicable, or not to hurt feelings unnecessarily. By the time the first volume of Segovia's memoirs was written, 1920 was over half a century distant – long enough to minimize the risk of such offense. There remains the chance of misrepresentation of the past, the result of faulty or 'selective' memory, and with it the likelihood of exposure by researchers in the archives, but this is a risk that is faced by every autobiographer. Dramatic revelations of untruth or inaccuracy are part of the fabric of investigative journalism, but they are important only if they show that history has given a specious account of the overall status and achievement of the central figure. At least some of the various misdemeanors of numerous historical figures, from Gesualdo to Paganini and Wagner, are now known (and had they lived today would have been of absorbing interest to readers of the down-market tabloids), but they do not affect our assessment of their achievements.

Only when his blue touchpaper was well and truly alight did he vent his displeasure on an offender; more often he was liable to convey it to a third party – he would have made a superb managing director! Nor can I remember more than one occasion on which he told me an anecdote, relating to any but his earliest years, in which the outcome was unfavorable to himself; his role was either that of the winner, or the unfortunate victim of circumstances. In this respect he was perhaps less unusual than in many others. It is difficult to assess the extent to which all these factors might have affected Segovia's account of his life, had it been completed, and impossible to know whether he ever really wished or intended to finish it anyway.

Some time after the text of this book was completed, it emerged that Segovia did indeed begin the second volume of his memoirs but the manuscript is brief and unedited. It was given to Graham Wade in order for him to show to his publisher as a 'trailer' – for a book that was not completed and will never be published.

Lunch at the Westbury Hotel, London, early 1980s, with two Andrés Segovias – on the left is his son, a painter who lives in Paris.

SUMMATION

In his youth, Andrés Segovia decided to devote his life to the classic guitar, setting himself a number of specific objectives: to rescue the guitar from its folk-musical, strumming image; to demonstrate its virtues by means of his concert tours, placing it alongside the piano, violin, and other 'established' instruments; to persuade places of tertiary musical education to include the serious study of the guitar in their curriculae; and to create a substantial, original repertory for it, by collaborating with notable composers. In his last years he expressed his satisfaction that they had been accomplished, though on one occasion he said to me, that the guitar's high popularity "might not last" – a private thought that, so far as I know, he never expressed publicly. He said this at the time when I had decided to cease to be a scientist, feeling that I might be exchanging a 'secure' income for one that could decline with the guitar's popularity, a characteristically considerate thought. [36] At that point, the guitar was at its apogee, and there was no obvious reason to doubt that it would continue to prosper. Certain question marks existed in the minds of the forward-thinking (including myself), if only that raised by the waxings and wanings of the instrument's popularity throughout its history; what evoked those in Segovia's mind, I do not know. It may be, that he felt that the guitar was 'identified' with *him* to such an extent that it might suffer recession after his death – he was then well into his seventies and could not have known that he would live almost two decades more. To what extent his messianic dreams were truly fulfilled, is open to question – the debating of which is outside the parameters of this little book, but without doubt he did go some way toward realizing them.

Comparable dreams could have entered the minds of other guitarists whose lives overlapped with Segovia's, some of whom were comparably gifted, musically and guitaristically, but only he had the strength of evangelistic purpose it needed to make them come, even partially, true. Never before or since has any musical instrument been so closely, and for so long, identified with a single performer. One 'badge of eminence' is awarded when an artist is known and billed by his surname alone – just 'Segovia,' and he remains the only classic guitarist who has been recognized in this way, worldwide. He was universally acclaimed and revered, and his experience of playing to full houses, to the.end of his life, was unique among guitarists. He brought to his on-stage deport-ment the dignity he wished to establish for the guitar itself. Every human being is three-dimensional (though some may appear more like cardboard cutouts than others!) and the dimensions of a great artist are likely to be greater than the average; it would be remarkable if any of those larger dimensions were free from flaws or limitations, inherent or self-inflicted. To portray *any* artist, even the greatest, as an unblemished paragon, one who never put a foot wrong or entertained an ignoble thought, and whose every utterance carried the authority of the Ten Commandments, would be to paint a picture that no thinking person could find credible. I have tried to flesh out more fully the 'image' of Andrés Segovia, presenting him as I found him, and giving a balanced measure of his dimensions. To have omitted the negatives that accompanied (and were far outweighed by) the positives, would have been naive or dishonest, neither serving historical truth nor doing Segovia justice. Exactly what were his achievements and his entitlements to immortality? I have my own answers to these questions but, more importantly, I hope I have added a little to the written stock of 'Segoviana,' and have helped each reader to come to his/her own conclusions.

On a page of Guitar Review No. 4, 1947. *Added a few years later:* "For Jacques Duarte with my sincere admiration and friendship."

Appendix I

The early
recordings

The playing on some tracks of the early (1927-1939) recordings sounds breathtakingly virtuosic, even by today's highest standards. Careful checking reveals, however, that, with perhaps one exception (the Mendelssohn *Canzonetta*), they also sound about one semitone above standard pitch. The present standard ('concert pitch') of A = 440 c.p.s. was internationally established only in 1939. During the preceding few decades it had varied from one country to another – but not sufficiently to account for a difference of a semitone: in England, where these recordings were made, it was in fact fractionally lower than 440. We cannot therefore explain the phenomenon in these terms. Another possibility is that Segovia then tuned his guitar about a semitone higher, performing these extraordinary feats of dexterity when his strings were at their tightest; this seems no less improbable.

As anyone who has ever set their record player at the wrong speed will know, the faster a disc is spun, the faster the speed of the music – and the higher its pitch. What does then seem more probable is, that the variation has its roots in the recordings themselves. If we correlate the pitch of the recordings with the dates on which they were made, we find that those tracks which were made during the sessions of 2/5/1927, 20/5/1927 and 15/5/1928 are the ones which emerge a semitone too high – with one mysterious exception, the *Fandanguillo* of Turina, which is markedly less than a semitone sharp! All these were held in the Small Queen's Hall (London), where also were those of 6-7/10/1930, in which the pitch is at, or very close to, normal. Did EMI install new, improved equipment between 1928 and 1930? They are now unable to answer the question. The remaining sessions (2/4/1935, 9/4/1935, 13/10/1936, 17/1/1939) were at EMI's Abbey Road studios (at first using equipment transferred from the Small Queen's Hall?), are associated with no abnormality of pitch, and thus reflect the true speeds at which the music was played.

It is tempting to attribute the high-pitched, high-speed tracks to some imprecision of running speed of the earliest recording equipment used, but there remains one other mystery: the LPs and CDs were reprocessed from tapes made from the original master discs – from which the 78s were pressed; I still have some of those 78s, purchased before World War II, and they too are at the higher pitch, suggesting that the discrepancy pre-dates the use of modern equipment in making the transfers and was probably caused by the inaccuracy or capriciousness of the early recording gear.

My own record player enables me to vary its speed continuously, not only in the usual steps – 33-45-78. When the semitone-high tracks are restored to normal pitch, they still sound impressive – but much more believable. If you, the reader, can do likewise, do so; it will give you a more truthful picture. There are similar problems in relation to the even earlier (c.1925) recordings of Miguel Llobet, [37] on which no information regarding venue(s) or date(s) is available. Dr. Ronald C. Purcell, who was involved in the remastering of the original recordings for the production of the LP issue, tells me that some of these were running as much as a *whole-tone* above today's pitch (and consequently sounding superhumanly fast); they adjusted the pitch/speeds of these downwards by a semitone but "didn't feel comfortable with stepping them back a whole-tone." He says also that: "Even if we were to have reduced the speed of the Coste *Studio brillante, Op. 38/22* by another semitone, metronome: crotchet = 176 is still flying along." These recordings of Llobet were made in Spain by Parlophone S.A. of Barcelona.

The recording details are not included in the annotation to either the LP or CD reissues of the 1927-1939 sessions; they are as follows – '+' signifies that the pitch and running speed are too high, A and B refer to the two sides of the LP discs, SQH = Small Queen's Hall, ARS = Abbey Road studio:

Item	Date	Venue	LP Disc	LP Track	CD Disc	CD Track	Pitch
Bach:							
Gavotte (from BWV 1006)	02/05/27	SQH	1A	1	1	1	+
Courante (from BWV 1009)	02/05/27	SQH	1A	2	1	2	+
Prélude (from BWV 1007)	09/04/35	ARS	1A	3	1	3	OK
Prélude BWV 999	15/05/28	SQH	1A	4a	1	4	+
Allemande (from BWV 996)	15/05/28	SQH	1A	4b	1	5	+
Fugue (from BWV 1001)	15/05/28	SQH	1A	5	1	6	+
Ponce/"Weiss":							
Suite in A	06/10/30	SQH	1A	6	1	7-10	OK
Sor:							
Thème varié, Op.9	02/05/27	SQH	1B	1	1	11	+
De Visée:							
Pieces in D minor	17/01/39	ARS	1B	2a	1	12-14	OK
Froberger:							
Gigue	17/01/39	ARS	1B	2b	1	15	OK
Torroba:							
Allegretto	20/05/27	SQH	1B	3	1	16	+
Mendelssohn:							
Canzonetta	13/10/36	ARS	1B	4	1	17	(+)
Malats: Serenata	06/10/30	SQH	1B	5	1	18	OK
Tárrega:							
Recuerdos	20/05/27	SQH	1B	6	1	19	+
Etude in A	09/04/35	ARS	1B	7	1	20	OK
Castelnuovo-Tedesco:							
Vivo ed energico	13/10/36	ARS	1B	8	1	21	OK
Albéniz:							
Granada	17/01/39	ARS	2A	1	2	1	OK
Sevilla	17/01/39	ARS	2A	2	2	2	OK
Torroba:							
Fandanguillo	15/05/28	SQH	2A	3	2	3	+
Preludio	15/05/28	SQH	2A	4	2	4	+
Nocturno	06/10/30	SQH	2A	5	2	5	OK
Turina:							
Fandanguillo	20/05/27	SQH	2A	6	2	6	+
Granados:							
Danza española No.10	17/01/39	ARS	2A	7	2	7	OK
Danza española No.5	17/01/39	ARS	2A	8	2	8	OK
Ponce:							
Sonata III/1	07/10/30	SQH	2B	1	2	9	OK
Canción	07/10/30	SQH	2B	2a	2	10	OK
Postlude	07/10/30	SQH	2B	2b	2	11	OK
Mazurka	07/10/30	SQH	2B	3	2	12	OK
Petite valse	09/04/35	ARS	2B	4	2	13	OK
Folies d'Espagne	06-07/10/30	SQH	2B	5	2	14	OK

Appendix II

The Segovia-Ponce
letters

Shortly after I completed the text of this book I received a copy of Miguel Alcázar's compilation of the letters sent by Segovia to Ponce – those, that is, which have survived (Editions Orphée, ISBN 0-936186-29-1 [38]). As this book has since been withdrawn in consequence of legal action, I cannot quote directly from it; I can indicate only what the letters tell us.

The pity is that they reveal only one side of the exchanges. Many letters Segovia received from Ponce were probably among the possessions Segovia had to abandon when he fled from Spain at the outbreak of the Civil War in 1938, but the book contained letters from Segovia dating as far forward as 1948, to which

Ponce is unlikely not to have replied. Alcázar suggests that they may have been lost as a result of Segovia's many changes of residence during those years; for whatever reason, they appear to be unavailable.

What emerges clearly is that to a significant extent Ponce and Segovia became interdependent. In Ponce, Segovia recognized the composer who was best equipped to provide him with repertory that was absolutely to his taste – and which the guitar needed; accordingly he pressed him relentlessly to fulfill the projects he (Segovia) envisaged, sometimes so strongly that he must have absorbed most of Ponce's creative time and effort. When Ponce was slow to respond to his letters and/or suggestions, Segovia feared that he had caused some offense and, as this might have meant the end of their collaboration, adopted a very conciliatory, even pleading stance. Ponce, on the other hand, suffered a prolonged period of hardship, in terms of both the development of his compositional career and the size of his income; Segovia, whose fame and financial well-being were growing rapidly at the time – albeit not without the occasional setback, assisted him with great generosity in both these things. Their relationship was thus very much to their mutual benefit, though it was Segovia who 'called the shots': he constantly bombarded Ponce with requests to write new pieces or to modify what he had already written, and Ponce did his level best to comply. Some projects were completed only slowly, *e.g.*, the Guitar Concerto, for which Segovia was already pressing in 1926 but which did not achieve its premiere until 1941; several others appear to have come to naught.

The letters throw a good deal of light on the genesis of many of the familiar major works. It appears that the original intention to precede the *Variations and Fugue on 'Las Folias'* with a Prelude was abandoned, but the footnote on pp. 130-31 is incorrect: at no time have I ever said that the *"Postlude"* which Segovia recorded in 1930 was the Prelude in question; in my annotation to the LP reissue of Segovia's early recordings I described it as a variation which, for some undisclosed reason, Segovia did not include in either the recording or the published edition, and this is exactly how he explained it to me. Segovia's accounts of past events sometimes varied from one telling to another – that fickle jade again – so that the total truth could only be guessed at! The famous *Suite in A*, for a long time attributed to Weiss, is a case in point. The fact that it was written by Ponce was known to many as early as the late 1950s, but Segovia was anxious that it should be suppressed, since he thought it might reflect adversely on all concerned, and even on the guitar. In the early 1970s, however, I had at short notice to write the programme notes for a recital in the Queen Elizabeth Hall by Alirio Diaz, in which one item was named as *"Suite antica"* by Ponce. Since I knew of no work by Ponce which bore that title I had no option but to assume it to be the "Weiss" Suite, and to acknowledge and explain it as such in the notes. Segovia had told me that the work was originally intended to be "by Bach" but, fearing that Bach's music was too thoroughly researched for them to get away with it, they changed the ascription, selecting (from an encyclopedia) the name of a German baroque lutenist who was then little known, the decision being taken when only the *Gigue* remained to be written. The *Gigue* is certainly materially different from the other movements in that it covers a far wider pitch-range, one that precludes any notion that it *could* have been a baroque-lute piece. Ironically, it was this work that spread Weiss' fame abroad, before lutenists were active enough to do it 'legitimately' on a significant scale. A letter of ca. 1936 reveals that Segovia was anxious to have another

Suite "by Weiss." Yet the first reference to the existing Suite is in a letter of December 1929, in which Segovia says that he had learnt it, with no mention of Bach in this or any other preserved letter dating back to 1923.

It is interesting, too, that whilst lavish (on occasion euphoric) in his praise of Ponce's music, Segovia was critical (in 1929) of the music of Turina, Manén, and even Torroba. What this seems to imply is, that Segovia *was* anxious to 'modernize' and extend the language of guitar music, a thing which he perceived Ponce's compositions as doing. At the same time there was a cut-off point, defined in musical terms rather than by the birth date of the composer: Turina (1882) and Manén (1883) looked to the past, Ponce was OK, but God preserve us and the guitar from Stravinsky (1882), Martin (1890) and Milhaud (1892)! To advance the language of music was admirable, indeed essential, but to depart from traditional concepts was not. On the cusp, as it were, there were those like Tansman, and in later years myself, who were able to set aside our more dissonant propensities 'to order,' wiping our pens clean when the occasion demanded it. Segovia's unreserved championing of Torroba in his last decades could hardly have been predicted from the comments in his early letters to Ponce! After Ponce's death (1948), Torroba seems to have become central to Segovia's affection for living composers (that for Ponce never wavered), though his musical style had not changed in the interim; apart from the loyalty/gratitude factor, the remembrance that Torroba had been the first to answer Segovia's pleas for new works in the 1920s, he was probably regarded also as a bulwark against the flood-tide of unpleasant modernism – and one who wrote romantic Spanish music. Rodrigo was fighting the same rear-guard action but he was fond of introducing gratuitous dissonance, and Segovia's personal relationship with him was not always a happy one. [39]

What may perhaps appear strange is, that, despite his connections with South America – and Argentina in particular, Segovia played so little of the music of that continent. However, he was averse to propagating overtly 'popular' music, unless the 'folk' elements were presented in European art-musical dress, giving them a cloak of respectability and dignity. This is what he perceived Ponce, and to a lesser extent Villa-Lobos, as doing. For the rest, I remember his statement to me, sometime in the late 1950s, that "South America is full of leetle musicians." He would not then have been aware of many of those we now know and love, but although many came to prominence in Segovia's later decades, he did not play their music. I do not even venture to guess why!

APPENDIX III

Addenda

There are two anecdotes which do not slot neatly into the main text, but are worth recording. Both relate to Segovia's 'green-room' experiences in South America; he did not name the countries concerned:

1) Two enthusiasts, after the usual complimentary 'bouquets,' asked: "Why did you play the Mendelssohn *(Canzonetta)* so fast?" He could have explained that the tempo was appropriate to the music, but instead he simply said: "Because I *can*!" In a broader

context this is of course the ultimate justification for displays of virtuosity: if you've got it, flaunt it – but if it's all you have, try not to let it show!

2) He was approached by a man who obviously knew, that Segovia's favorite strings at that time were of a brand that was then extremely difficult to come by. The man told him he had several sets of them. Segovia asked how much he would accept for them, but he was told they were not for sale. The man had had what was no doubt his greatest moment of squalid glory: He had denied the great Segovia of something he dearly wanted – and he could have given to him. Venomous life was not to be found only in jungles.

TEXT REFERENCES

(1) Once, having a tape recorder with me for another purpose, I taped part of a conversation that seemed particularly interesting; however it veered in another and very personal direction, and Segovia, seeing the recorder running, said: "I hope you will erase that." I did not do so, but it will not be found in this book.

(2) HMV RLS 745 (2 LPs).

(3) One movement, the *Larghetto*, is published by Columbia Music (CO 153).

(4) HMV HLM 134 (LP, mono). Testament SBT 1043 (CD).

(5) *Guitar Review* No.12 (1951).

(6) *Guitar Review* No.11 (1951). Broekmans & Van Poppel 937.

(7) When in the early 1950s my name began to be known in other countries, I reverted to my given name of "John" in order to minimize this confusion. Nevertheless, in 1996 I am still asked from time to time, whether I am related to one or the other!

(8) MCA MUCS 125.

(9) How early is 'early'? 'Authentic' performance practice has now reached well into the nineteenth century! What characterizes all so-called 'early' music is, that we can never be 100% sure of how it was played and sounded in its own time; musicology brings us ever closer to the answers but it can never bring us to complete certainty. However, music that was *recorded* in the lifetime of a composer (especially when performed or conducted by the composer) can never be 'early' as long as there is power to drive a reproducer. The music of, for instance, Chopin, Schumann and Wagner will always be 'early, but that of Stravinsky, Ravel and Britten never can be. The watershed is thus the invention of the gramophone. Later generations may not like the way earlier music was played in its own time, but they cannot plead ignorance!

(10) RCA ARL1 8864 (LP).

(11) When Stravinsky asked Segovia why he had never asked him for a piece for the guitar, the answer was: "Because I do not want to insult your music by not playing it." I am not the only one to whom he told this anecdote!

(12) Julian Bream persuaded him to change his mind, but Martin died before he could write again for the guitar.

(13) Published by Tecla Editions.

(14) *"Le but de cette leçon est d'habituer l'écolier à donner au pouce de la main droite la véritable direction, en le faisant alterner avec l'index pour les triples croches."* "The object of this study is to accustom the student to giving the right-hand thumb its correct direction, by making it alternate with the index finger in playing the thirty-second notes (demi-semi-quavers)." In the

Segovia edition the right-hand fingering is given as *a.i.m.i.m*, instead of the original *p.i.p.i.p*, which was established from the earliest times as a means of playing repeated notes or passagework. Exactly when and by whom this earlier form of fingering was discarded, would make a useful subject for a thesis. As a useful resource, it has been resurrected in the second half of the present century. We now have both the baby and the bath water!

(15) *Guitar Review* No.31 (1969) p.3.

(16) Ed. Vladimir Bobri, Macmillan (1972).

(17) Collins (1979).

(18) Tecla Editions (1981).

(19) For many decades, if one asked someone what had prompted their interest (active or passive) in the classic guitar, the answer was almost invariably: "I heard Segovia." If they were then asked what it was about his playing that they found most appealing, it was: "the beautiful variety of sounds he produces." The "miniature orchestra," as Beethoven is said to have described the guitar.

(20) Published by Novello.

(21) *Guitar Review* No.11 (1950).

(22) Novello.

(23) Published by Berben, E1717B.

(24) Novello.

(25) Berben, E2366B.

(26) Published by Zanibon, 5758, 5759, 5761.

(27) Novello.

(28) Novello.

(29) Tecla Editions (1981).

(30) *Guitar Review* No.31 (1969)

(31) *Ibid.*

(32) On one occasion when, having bought two or three new dress suits, he had overestimated the capacity of his baggage, he arrived at our home carrying the suit he was currently using, and asked if we would store it for him. We reminded him of it on later visits but he evinced no interest in recovering it, so we eventually let the matter rest. It still hangs in my wardrobe, an ongoing reminder of wonderful times past.

(33) RCA Red Seal RL 12602 (LP).

(34) EMI Références CHS 761047 2 (2 CDs).

(35) Decca Gold Label DL 710179 (Vol.1). MCA DL 710182 (Vol.2).

(36) Whatever doubts he and I may have entertained in 1969, they have proved unjustified. I have never had the slightest reason to regret changing professional horses in mid-stream, nor have I once looked back on my life as a scientist with nostalgia!

(37) El Maestro EM 8003 (LP), Chanterelle (cassette).

(38) Editions Orphée, ISBN 0-936186-29-1 (withdrawn from publication).

(39) This was made very clear in our conversations but it would be improper to elaborate by quoting (let alone from memory!) the incidents Segovia described to me.

INDEX OF NAMES

Kennedy, President John: 73
Koshkin, Nikita: 47-48
Kreisler, Fritz: 28
Landowska, Wanda: 31, 44
Legnani, Luigi: 70
Llobet, Miguel: 82, 122
Mace, Thomas: 61
Malats, Joaquin: 123
Manén, Juan: 46, 127
Martin, Frank: 46, 127, 132
Martinez, Dr. Alex: 112
Medtner, Nikolay: 71
Mendelssohn, Felix: 30, 120, 123, 129
Mikulka, Vladimir: 47
Milhaud, Darius: 47, 127
Mills, John: 48
Mitchell, Joan: 17
Montgomery, Wes: 65
Mozart, W.A.: 30, 63
Mudarra, Alonso: 40
Paganini, Nícolo: 69-70, 115
Pedrell, Felipe: 26
Peijel, Cecilia: 36, 69
Perlman, Ithzak: 69
Picasso, Pablo: 22
Ponce, Manuel: 43, 46, 71, 74-77, 79, 123-8
Presti, Ida: 50, 56-57, 82, 89-90
Pujol, Emilio: 32, 39, 82, 90
Purcell, Dr. Ronald: 122
Rachmaninov, Sergei: 28, 71
Ramirez, Manuel: 88
Ravel, Maurice: 46, 132
Ricci, Ruggero: 69
Robles, Marisa: 70
Rodrigo, Joaquin: 46, 65-66, 127-128
Romero, Pepe: 98
Rossini, Giacomo: 30
Roussel, Albert: 47
Rubenstein, Artur: 107

Sanz, Gaspar: 39
Scarlatti, Domenico: 29, 38, 100
Schoenberg, Arnold: 46
Schubert, Franz: 27
Schumann, Robert: 132
Segovia, Andrés III: 113, 116
Segovia, Beatriz: 25
Segovia, Carlos Andrés: 86, 94, 113-114
Segovia, Emilia (Emilita): 20-21, 23, 67, 93-94, 107, 110, 113
Sor, Fernando: 4, 11, 30, 49-50, 55, 123, 132
Stravinsky, Igor: 46, 127, 132
Tansman, Alexandre: 46, 70, 77, 106, 127
Tárrega, Francisco: 4, 28, 30, 33, 53-4, 123
Tillett, Emmie: 99
Tippett, Sir Michael: 79
Tomas, José: 37
Torres, Antonio: 4
Torroba, Federico Moreno: 46, 72, 77, 98, 123, 127
Turina, Joaquin: 26, 46, 77, 121, 123, 127
Usher, Terence: 7-8, 11-16, 18, 63, 95, 108
Villa-Lobos, Heitor: 13, 128
Viñes, Ricardo: 66
Visée, Robert de: 29, 47, 123
Wade, Graham: 116
Wagner, Richard: 115, 132
Walton, Sir William: 79
Watson, Michael: 20
Weiss, Leopold Sylvius: 126-127
Williams, John: 18-20, 28, 69, 91-93
Williams, Len: 18
Williams, Melaan: 18-19
Ysäe, Eugène: 28
Zabaleta, Nicanor: 70